Oracle® SQL Developer's Guide

Oracle® SQL Developer's Guide

Carolyn J. Hursch
Jack L. Hursch

NOTICES

IBM® **DB2™** **IMS™** **SQL/DS™**	International Business Machines Corp.
ORACLE® **SQL*DBA™** **SQL*FORMS™** **SQL*GRAPH™** **SQL*LOADER™** **SQL*Menu™** **SQL*NET™** **SQL*REPORT™** **SQL*STAR™** **SQL*PLUS™** **PL/SQL™** **PRO*C™**	Oracle Corp.

FIRST EDITION
FIRST PRINTING

Library of Congress Cataloging-in-Publication Data

Hursch, Carolyn J.
Oracle SQL developer's guide / by Carolyn J. Hursch and Jack L. Hursch.
p. cm.
Includes bibliographical references and index.
ISBN 0-8306-2566-6 (h) ISBN 0-8306-2529-1 (p)
1. SQL (Computer program language) 2. Oracle (Computer file)
I. Hursch, Jack L. II. Title.
QA76.73.S67H86 1991
005.75′65—dc20 91-15491
CIP

TAB Books offers software for sale. For information and a catalog, please contact TAB Software Department, Blue Ridge Summit, PA 17294-0850.

Acquisitions Editor: Ron Powers
Technical Editor: Patti McCarty
Production: Katherine G. Brown
Book Design: Jaclyn J. Boone
Cover: Sandra Blair Design, Harrisburg, PA WPT1

Contents

Introduction

The widespread implementation of relational databases has brought with it the need for a database language that is user-friendly enough for the casual user, yet convenient for the programmer and applications builder. The Structured Query Language, SQL (pronounced "sequel"), after a rapid period of evolution, fills that need. An end user can learn to use it easily and the programmer can embed SQL in procedural languages such as C, Cobol, or PL/1.

The SQL language provides a much-needed common avenue of discourse between the end-user and the programmer. This fact alone provides substantial benefit in smoothing out the transition from paper files to computerized database systems, and in the development of applications for existing database systems.

This text sets forth the structure and syntax of SQL as it is used in Oracle Corporation's relational database management system (RDBMS) called ORACLE, along with all the modifications and enhancement that Oracle has added over time to increase the power of standard SQL as presented by the American National Standards Institute (ANSI). This then is ANSI standard SQL with many enhancements added by Oracle Corporation. The result is presented here in sufficient detail for anyone involved with an ORACLE RDBMS—from the casual user to the computer professional—to quickly learn and make use of ORACLE's SQL to create, maintain, and query a database of any size.

Exercises making use of everyday situations, at the end of most chapters, should help you develop a hands-on familiarity with SQL in ORACLE.

In order to present the complete picture of SQL, we also trace its mathematical structure from its basis in first-order logic to its present-day role as one of the most popular structured query language in the world of commercial database management systems. The chapters that work through this process are set apart from the detailed description of the SQL language because they might be of more interest to computer science professionals than to the user who is trying to gain a working knowledge of SQL in ORACLE. The contents of the text are as follows.

CHAPTER 1 traces the history of the development of SQL from E.F. Codd's articles in the early 1970s, setting forth the principles of a relational database, through the D.D. Chamberlin articles of the late 1970s, to the latest publications of the American National Standards Institute (ANSI) in their efforts to develop a standard SQL language, and the latest enhancements to the language contained in Oracle's version of SQL.

CHAPTER 2 sets forth the notation and defines the terms used throughout the book.

CHAPTER 3 shows the basics of both SQL and ORACLE's user interface, which is called SQL*PLUS (pronounced "Sequel-plus").

CHAPTER 4 contains an overview of all of the components of conventional SQL language, the SQL commands, keywords, datatypes and value expressions supported by SQL. The three main types of statements—Data Definition, Data Manipulation, and Data Control—are listed and the syntax for each is shown as well as the syntax for the various expressions, connectives, predicates, and functions that make up the SQL language.

CHAPTER 5 contains explanations and examples of the use of SQL table expressions and predicates in preparation for using them in SQL commands.

CHAPTER 6 shows the use of logical connectives, SQL functions and subqueries as they are employed in ORACLE SQL, and includes examples of the use of NOT with each of these.

CHAPTER 7 illustrates the use of the Data Definition Statements CREATE, ALTER, and DROP, and gives examples of these statements as they are used to define and modify tables in an illustrative database system.

CHAPTER 8 illustrates the use of the Data Manipulation commands INSERT, UPDATE, DELETE, and SELECT. Because creating views (unlike creating tables) involves data manipulation, it is included in this chapter.

CHAPTER 9 explains the use of the Data Control Statements, by the persons who must administer the database, and discusses the security and integrity constraints that may be invoked using ORACLE SQL.

CHAPTER 10 is devoted exclusively to joins because joins can add a great deal to the efficient use of a relational database. Equijoins and non-equijoins are explained, as well as the Cartesian product, natural joins, and outer joins.

CHAPTER 11 discusses views in detail. With a well-designed database, the end user will be using views most of the time rather than base tables. At the same time, not all operations possible with tables are possible with views. Therefore, SQL operations on views are explained and the view-update problem is discussed. In chapter 11, the use of indices is discussed. This leads to a discussion of the optimal formation of queries in order to speed up the retrieval process.

CHAPTER 12 presents embedded SQL, a form of SQL that can be embedded in computer programs and converted to host language code with a precompiler. *Cursors* (implementor-defined work areas for holding relational tables obtained from queries) are discussed, as well as the embedded SQL commands for manipulating cursors. Suggestions are made for modifying the embedding process to make the programmer's task less onerous and produce bugfree programs. These suggestions are demonstrated by examples of SQL embedded in short C language modules that the programmer can modify to fit his or her own implementation and requirements.

CHAPTER 13 illustrates the use of PL/SQL, a procedural programming language developed by Oracle Corporation, that can be used with the ORACLE RDBMS. This chapter gives examples of how PL/SQL can be used with SQL commands.

SQL has been said to "resemble" tuple relational calculus. However, it contains properties taken from both relational algebra and relational calculus. Therefore, in chapter 14 the elements of relational algebra are developed and related to SQL.

CHAPTER 15 develops the elements of first-order logic needed for tuple relational calculus as discussed by E.F. Codd in an early article. Interpretations as developed in propositional calculus and predicate calculus with quantifiers are explained, and their extension in predicate calculus to a database scheme is exhibited. This database scheme is then shown to be an interpretation determining a form of predicate calculus known as *tuple relational calculus*. The extension of the idea of an interpretation is shown to determine what is retrieved by means of a query formulated in tuple relational calculus. Finally, the examples and exercises show how tuple relational calculus queries are converted to SQL queries. Thus, chapter 15 demonstrates the theme by which SQL developed from the need for a query language through first-order logic to a user-friendly relational database interface.

The Glossary defines all words peculiar to SQL in ORACLE, as well as all relational database terms that the reader might need to know in connection with this topic.

The Bibliography provides the interested reader with additional sources of information on all of the topics covered.

1
CHAPTER

How SQL got here

The popularity of the Structured Query Language, SQL (pronounced "sequel"), as a user-friendly interface to a relational database management system (RDBMS) has continued to grow at a rapid rate.

Even more impressive is the variety of innovations in the SQL language brought forth by the commercial relational database management systems now on the market. Foremost among these is that produced by Oracle Corporation, one of the leaders in the use of SQL in relational database management systems.

The original standards set forth by the American National Standards Institute (ANSI) for a SQL standard have now been augmented by new publications (ANSI X3.135-1989 and ANSI X3.168-1989), and the ANSI staff and associates continue to work toward further refinements of terms and concepts. At the same time, Oracle Corporation has gone far beyond the ANSI standard in its enhancements to SQL. Unlike some other commercial systems where SQL is an option, or an add-on to an existing database system, the ORACLE RDBMS and SQL are an integrated whole. As one of the first uses of SQL in a commercial database management system, ORACLE is built around the SQL data sublanguage. The advantage of this is that once the user knows SQL, he or she has a usable working knowledge of ORACLE.

This text, then, presents SQL in ORACLE, with all its enhancements, which also include the features contained in ANSI standard SQL.

First, however, it might be of interest to briefly discuss the developments that brought SQL to the point where it could be implemented within a relational database management system.

Roots

Here is a brief history of the development of the SQL data sublanguage. When E.F. Codd introduced the concept of a relational database in 1970, he suggested that "the adoption of a relational model of data . . . permits the development of a universal data sublanguage based on an applied predicate calculus." Although he indicated the requirements and the advantages of such a language, he did not attempt at that time to devise one. In a later article, he discussed the concept of "relational completeness"—a term that he coined, which is now widely used—of a database sublanguage.

Acceptance of the relational idea was relatively slow, although only in comparison with the usual speed of technical advances in the computer field. Therefore, it was not until 1974 that D.D. Chamberlin and R.F. Boyce published an article suggesting the form of a structured query language, which at that time was called SEQUEL. The following year, Boyce, Chamberlin, W.F. King, and M.M. Hammer published an article setting forth the sublanguage SQUARE which was much like SEQUEL except that SQUARE used mathematical expressions rather than the English terms of SEQUEL. Both languages are shown by the authors to be relationally complete in the sense outlined by Codd in his 1970 and 1972 articles. Relationally complete in this context means "at least as powerful as the tuple relational calculus."

The SQUARE article was followed by another article by Chamberlin and others in 1976 when the name was changed to SEQUEL 2, and it was used as the query language for the IBM research database System R.

By the time Chamberlin wrote an article in 1980 summarizing user experience with the language, the name had been changed to its present form: SQL, denoting a "Structured Query Language." A test of SQL by a broad group of users resulted in several changes to the language including the addition of "outer joins" to SQL's capabilities, which Codd had already suggested in his 1979 article. Further development reported in other articles resulted in present-day SQL. (See the Bibliography for complete references for all publications mentioned here.)

During the last decade, relational databases have emerged and become more popular than the hierarchical and network databases that preceded them. This trend appears to be accelerating.

Fully relational databases

To inject some order into the rapidly increasing literature on relational databases, Codd in 1985 laid down 12 principles, at least six of which must be satisfied in order for a database to call itself "fully relational." These were preceded by one overall general rule, called "Rule Zero" as follows:

Rule Zero For any system that is advertised as, or claimed to be, a relational database management system, that system must be able to manage databases entirely through its relational capabilities.

The essence of the 12 specific rules are as follows:

1. *Representation of information.* All information in a relational database is represented explicitly at the logical level and in exactly one way—by values in tables.
2. *Guaranteed logical accessibility.* Each and every datum (atomic value) in a relational database is guaranteed to be logically accessible by resorting to a combination of the table name, primary key value, and column name.
3. *Systematic representation of missing information.* Null values (distinct from the empty character string or a string of blank characters and distinct from zero or any other number) are supported in a fully relational DBMS for representing missing information and inapplicable information in a systematic way independent of datatype.
4. *Dynamic online catalog.* The database description is represented at the local level in the same way as ordinary data, so that authorized users can query it in the same relational language that they use in working with the regular data.
5. *Comprehensive data sublanguage.* A relational system may support several languages and various modes of terminal use, for example the fill-in-the-blanks mode. However, there must be at least one language whose statements are expressible, in some well-defined syntax, as character strings. Also, it must be comprehensive in supporting all of the following items:

    - Data definition
    - View definition
    - Data manipulation (interactive and by program)
    - Integrity constraints
    - Authorization
    - Transaction boundaries (begin, commit, and rollback)

6. *Updatable views.* All views that are theoretically updatable are also updatable by the database system.
7. *High-level insert, update, and delete.* The capability of handling a base relation or a derived relation as a single operand applies not only to retrieving data but also to inserting, updating, and deleting of data.
8. *Physical data independence.* Application programs and terminal activities remain logically unimpaired whenever any changes are made in either storage representations or access methods.
9. *Logical data independence.* Application programs and terminal activities remain logically unimpaired when information preserving appropriate changes of any kind are made to the base tables.
10. *Integrity independence.* Integrity constraints specific to a particular database must be definable in the relational data sublanguage and storable in the catalog, not in the application program.
11. *Distribution independence.* Whether or not a system supports database distribution, it must have a data sublanguage that can support distributed databases without impairing the application programs or terminal activities.
12. *Nonsubversion.* If a relational system has a low-level (single-record-at-a-time) language, that low-level language cannot be used to subvert or bypass the integrity rules and constraints expressed in the higher level relational language (multiple-records-at-a-time).

A proof that SQL is relationally complete has been outlined by C.J. Date (p. 276 of Date's *An Introduction to Database Systems*, Vol. 1).

Chapter 15 of this book gives a discussion of tuple relational calculus beginning with classical logic and in this development we demonstrate the conversion of logic queries to SQL.

The fact that the developers knew ahead of time what SQL should be and what it would be required to do, gave it a strong theoretical foundation. This is probably a first in computer language development because most computer languages in use today are the result of a basic idea supplemented by a great deal of ad hoc patching to meet problems as they arise. This fact—of specifying the need for SQL before developing the mechanics of it—gave rise to an elegantly parsimonious language consisting of relatively few commands that can be used to satisfy most of the needs of a very complex database.

Its simplicity makes SQL convenient for the casual user as well as the sophisticated developer. It can be used for ad hoc queries, and, it also can be embedded in a host-language program.

At this point, there are several structured languages in existence that are being used for querying relational databases. However, SQL appears to be the one most widely adopted for commercial use.

Current status

The American National Standards Institute (ANSI) has published a standard, called *Database Language SQL*, setting forth the minimal syntax and semantics for SQL. The ANSI standard uses the Backus-Naur Form (BNF) of syntactic notation which, for the reader's convenience, is not used here. (See Nauer, P. in the Bibliography for additional information.)

In its most recent publication (X3.135-1989), ANSI added an "integrity enhancement feature" to its original SQL standard. This feature demands that a database have some means for specifying referential constraints between tables, check constraints to be applied to the rows of a table, and a default value for a column when a row is inserted into a table.

(You can obtain the publication containing the current ANSI SQL standard (ANSI X3.135-1989) and any subsequent additions to that standard by contacting the American National Standards Institute, Inc., 1430 Broadway, New York, NY 10018. The ANSI phone number is 212-642-4900.)

Additional standards for the SQL language are planned by ANSI; topics now under consideration to be published as addenda to the existing standard are: referential integrity, enhanced transaction management, specification of certain user-defined rules, enhanced character handling facilities, and support for national character sets.

In keeping with the present trend, the National Institute of Standards and Technology (NIST) now has an Object-Oriented Database Task Group (OODBTG) working on a standard for an object-oriented SQL. At this writing, work has not progressed far enough for us to report on it, but this holds promise for the future.

Over the years, industry changes have been made in SQL due to product testing, user input, and further development. One of the most extensive uses of SQL is that in the ORACLE relational database management system (RDBMS). A pioneer in the use of the SQL language, Oracle Corporation has gone on to greatly enhance the original SQL language. In the ORACLE RDBMS, which can be used on many different platforms ranging from microcomputers to mainframes, the SQL language is an integral part of the system.

ORACLE also has used the SQL language as the basis for its user-friendly interface in an extension of SQL called SQL*Plus. This interface is discussed in detail in later chapters. In addition, the complete ORACLE RDBMS includes a number of utilities, all of which are SQL based. These include the SQL*DBA, SQL*Forms, SQL*Loader, SQL*Menu, SQL*Net, SQL*Report, and SQL*STAR. Some of these will be referred to briefly in the pages that follow. More information on all of them is available in publications of the Oracle Corporation at Belmont, California.

Summary

This chapter traces the development of SQL from its beginnings in the early 1970s to the adoption of standards for its use by ANSI, and the plans for further standardization by ANSI, as well as the object-oriented standards now being considered by NIST. The enhancements to SQL that occur within the ORACLE RDBMS are noted.

2
CHAPTER

Notations and definitions

This chapter explains the notation used in this book and defines the terms that are used throughout. The following notation will be used:

SQL Commands in caps. All SQL commands will be written in capital letters, for example: CREATE TABLE

Angle brackets (< >) to indicate what you must fill in. Angle brackets enclose a general term describing the specific term that you must fill in. For example, when you see the following:

```
CREATE TABLE <tablename>
```

you will need to fill in the name of a table from your own installation. (Do not put the angle brackets around the table name when you fill it in.)

Asterisk (*) to mean "all." An asterisk (*) has its usual meaning in computer practice—"all cases fitting the description." For example:

```
SELECT *
FROM <tablename>;
```

is interpreted as "select all columns from the named table."

Square brackets ([ ]) *to indicate an option.* Square brackets indicate that the term inside them is optional. For example:

```
SELECT <target list>
FROM <clause>
[WHERE <clause>];
```

means that you have the option of adding a WHERE clause to the commands listed. (Do not put the square brackets around the optional term if you do choose to use it in a SQL statement.)

Ellipses to indicate continuation. Ellipses will be used to indicate the continuation of a series, such as:

```
column1, column2, ..., columnN
```

which is interpreted as "column 1, column 2, and any other numbered columns, in order, to the end of the list of columns."

Words in a character string joined by an underscore. So that the host language will interpret them as a single character string, two or more adjacent words will be connected by an underscore whenever they are to be displayed as a table or column heading, as in:

```
employee_name
```

Slash (/) to indicate a choice. A slash within an expression is used to indicate that you have a choice between two or more given possibilities. For example:

```
ALL/ANY
```

means that you may choose either one of the terms ALL or ANY.

Semicolon as terminator for SQL statements. Every SQL statement must be ended with an implementor-defined termination symbol. In the ORACLE RDBMS every SQL statement must end with a semicolon (;).

Definitions

In keeping with the fact that SQL is an adjunct to a relational database management system, the following terms are defined within the relational context.

Relations

In 1971, E.F. Codd introduced the idea of using "tables" as the main database structure. He described a table as a rectangular array with the following properties:

- A table is column-homogeneous. In other words, in any selected column the items must all be the same kind. Items in different columns, however, do not need to be the same kind.

- Each item is a simple number or a character string. (Thus, for example, if you look at the item in any specified row and any specified column, you do not find a set of numbers or a group.)

For database tables, there are three more properties:

- All rows of a table must be distinct (duplicate rows are not allowed).
- The ordering of rows within a table is immaterial.
- The columns of a table are assigned distinct names, and the ordering of columns within a table is immaterial.

This kind of table is called a *relation*. If it has *n* columns, then it is called a *relation of degree n*.

Relation schemes

Column names are called *attributes*. The set of all column names for a table is called a *relation scheme*; and the table is a "relation over the relation scheme." In general, a database consists of more than one table, each having its own set of attributes or column names. The *database scheme* is the collection of all relation schemes of tables in the database. (Two distinct relation schemes may have some column names (attributes) in common.) A table is an *instance* of a relation over a relation scheme, for example if you change the data in the table in any way you have a different relation with the same relation scheme. Chapter 14 gives further details on the distinction between a relation scheme and a relation.

To summarize these definitions and relate them to the terms used in this text:

- A table will be called a *relation*
- An attribute will be called a *column*
- A single record will be called a *row*
- An individual value at the intersection of any row and column will be called a *datum*

Databases

A *database* is a set of dictionary tables and user tables that are treated as a unit. A *database system* may consist of a large number of individual databases, each with its own name.

Tables

A *table* in a relational database system is a named row of column headings, with zero or more rows of data values inserted under those headings. Its uses do not all have to be established before entering the data. Tables are the basic units of a relational database system.

A table name may be preceded by the name of the person who created it, followed by a period. For example, a table called Personnel created by Barber may be referred to as Barber.Personnel or simply by the name Personnel.

A table name may not be a SQL reserved word (SQL reserved words are listed in chapter 4).

There are two types of tables in a relational database: base tables and virtual tables. A *base table* conforms to the definition of a table just given. A *virtual table*, also called a *view*, exists only as a definition in the *catalog*. (The catalog is described in chapter 4.) Every time a view is accessed, the definition is retrieved from the catalog and the query in the definition is executed, creating a new table with the columns listed in the view definition. A view is called a *virtual table* because it does not exist in its own right in the database as a base table does. Instead, a view is reconstructed from the data of its underlying base table(s) whenever the view is queried.

Base tables are usually referred to simply as "tables"; the full name "base tables" is used here to distinguish them from "virtual tables" which are discussed below. Throughout this text, base tables will simply be called "tables" and virtual tables will be called "views."

A base table must have a name. You must assign this name to it when you set it up using the CREATE TABLE command (explained in chapter 4). A base table exists in its own right in the database, whether or not it will ever be retrieved in that form. A base table can be altered or dropped which will result in the altering or dropping of all indices and views defined on it.

Virtual tables (views)

A table that does not exist in its own right in the database, but looks to the user as though it does, is called a *virtual table*. For example, in answer to a query, a table might appear on the screen that is only part of a base table, such as the list of names of all employees whose annual salary is under $50,000. That table as such might not exist in the database; however, a base table showing all employees, their salaries, and a great deal of other information about them might actually exist in the database. Therefore, the appropriate SQL command will produce a virtual table where only those name-and-salary combinations under $50,000 are available.

A view is a virtual table. It is a look at a portion of the data that has been retrieved from one or more base tables. A view is a named, derived table. It is a "window" into one or more base tables.

In its simplest form, a view can be a portion of a base table but it also can be the result of joining a portion of one or more tables together. And there's another possibility: a view can be a portion of a view, with the latter view being a portion of a base table. Views are discussed in detail in chapter 11.

Views allow for data independence. In multi-user systems, views allow the same data to be seen by different users in different contexts—all at the same time. Forcing users to work only with views can provide automatic security for hidden data in the base tables. It also can be faster, and more efficient, for end users to bring up only the information they need in concise form rather than a huge base table full of information that they do not need (and perhaps should not see) each time they need to work with the database.

In a large multi-user system, most users will usually be working with views rather than base tables.

Columns

A *column name* is the name that you, the user, give to represent the data values that will be entered under it. The columns of a table in a relational database system have the following properties: (1) Each column of a table has a unique name in that table; and (2) the columns in a table are ordered from left to right, for example Column 1, Column 2...Column *n*. (Although, from a mathematical standpoint, the second statement is not strictly true because in a relational system the columns are unordered. However, from the user's point of view, the order in which the column names are entered becomes the order in which value entries must be entered, unless the column is named each time a record is entered.)

Rows

The rows can be seen as representing the records in a file, so we use the terms "rows" and "records" interchangeably. The rows of a table in a relational database have the following properties:

- Rows are unordered, unless for the user's convenience, an ordering is imposed on a set of rows when they are retrieved, but such an ordering is not intrinsic to the table.
- Each row of a table has only one value for each column of that table.
- All rows of a table have the same set of columns although any row may have NULL values in specific columns—it may have no value for those columns.
- Each row of a table must be unique.

Data values

An individual data value, for example, the value found at the intersection of a column and row, will be defined here as a *datum*. Some database systems refer to the individual value at the intersection of a row and column as "data" and also refer to the entire set of entries in the table as "data." When we refer to an individual entry, we will use the word datum, the singular form of "data."

Some database systems call the individual value a "field" and some refer to the entire column as a field. We will call each individual value a datum and the individual place in the column where that datum is entered will be called a *field*.

Target list

The desired list of columns in a query, the list of columns appearing after the SELECT command, will be called the *target list*. This is in keeping with Codd's usage of that term in tuple relational calculus.

NULL values

A NULL value is a missing datum. It is not necessarily equal to zero or to any other value. One NULL value is not necessarily equal to any other NULL value.

For some columns in a table, NULL values should not be allowed to occur. In other words, in any database, there is some information too vital to be left blank if the row is filled in at all. You can prevent these blank spaces in your tables by specifying NOT NULL when you create the vital column. This specification ensures that the necessary datum will not be omitted when a record is entered into the database. Columns containing important identifiers, such as Social Security numbers, which if omitted would cause a serious handicap to the whole operation, should be specified as NOT NULL. On the other hand, a column specified as NOT NULL will not accept a record with a missing value in that column with the promise that it will be filled in later. Therefore, judicious use of the specification is necessary. (Fortunately, there are ways to get around this problem; the Null Value Function (NVL) explained in the next section is one such solution.)

ORACLE SQL supports the concept of a NULL value to indicate incomplete or unavailable information. This value can be thought of as simply a placeholder in the domain of an attribute. (For this reason, E.F. Codd suggests in his 1990 book that the name "mark" be substituted for NULL to point up the fact that it is merely a mark, not a value. However, at this writing the suggestion has not yet taken hold to any appreciable degree in the industry. Therefore, we will continue to use the term NULL in this text.)

There are differing opinions about the utility or indeed the logic behind the concept of NULL values, as for example, in the following references: C.J. Date (See chapter 15 in *Relational Database: Selected Writings*), W. Lipski, Jr. (September 1979 paper), Codd (in his December 1979 ACM paper and 1990 book) and D. Maier (in his section on NULLs).

However, at the present time, NULLs are very much a part of SQL and appear more likely to be modified and embellished than eliminated from its syntax in the future. They serve the purpose of filling in a blank space in the array of data, but they must be used with caution. The following rules apply (other special uses and cautions about NULLs will be noted in the contexts where they occur):

- A NULL value is not the same as a zero.
- One NULL value is not necessarily equal to another NULL value.
- Treatment of NULLs by each of the aggregate functions is not uniform (See chapter 6).

The NULL value function (NVL)

To attack the problems presented by NULLs occurring in the database, the ORACLE relational database system has implemented a Null Value Function (NVL). With NVL you can convert a NULL entry in a field to a specified non-NULL entry for the purpose of evaluating an expression. For example, if a company employs personnel who receive commissions as well as personnel who do not, then a NULL in the commission column of a table, for an employee who does not receive commissions, could be replaced by a zero. In the ORACLE system, NVL requires two arguments: an expression and a non-null value. The syntax is:

```
NVL <x,expr>
```

The value of the NVL approach is especially apparent when dealing with aggregate functions, which are discussed in chapter 6.

Reserved words

Reserved words are words that are not available to the user for use as names of tables, columns or views. If you should use a reserved word for the name of a table, column or view, you will get an error message to the effect that the word you used "is not a valid name." In ORACLE SQL however, you may use a reserved word for a name if you enclose it in double quotes, for example, "DATABASE." A list of ORACLE SQL reserved words appears in chapter 4.

Database objects

Individual databases within a system, as well as the tables, views, indices, synonyms, aliases, columns, and rows are all called *database objects*. When this term occurs, it refers to one or more of these entities, with its exact meaning made clear by the context.

Result tables

The answer to any SQL query will appear on your screen in the form of a table. This is called a *result table*.

Summary

This chapter illustrates the notation used through this book. It also defines the relational database terms that are necessary in explaining the use of SQL in ORACLE.

3
CHAPTER

SQL and SQL*Plus

The Structured Query Language (SQL) is the interface between the user and the ORACLE database. It was originally defined by a group at the IBM research laboratory in San Jose, California. It is both an interactive query language, and a database programming language. Its interactive properties are discussed in this chapter. Its use as a programming language is discussed in chapter 13 under the title PL/SQL.

SQL*Plus is an interactive command-driven interface to ORACLE, used for querying and report writing. It was developed by the Oracle Corporation.

The SQL language

SQL consists of four main types of statements:

- Data Definition Statements (DDS)
- Data Manipulation Statements (DMS)
- Queries
- Data Control Statements (DCS)

The first three types are used by all users to create and maintain the database. The fourth type, Data Control Statements (DCS) are used mainly by the database administrator to grant access to the database, and to institute and maintain security procedures. The four types are described as follows.

Data Definition Statements (DDS) The Data Definition Statements (DDS) such as CREATE TABLE, CREATE VIEW, CREATE SYNONYM, ALTER TABLE, DROP TABLE, DROP VIEW, DROP SYNONYM, and DROP INDEX are used to set up and maintain the database. The syntax of these statements is shown in chapter 4 and examples of them are in chapter 7.

Data Manipulation Statements (DMS) The Data Manipulation Statements (DMS) such as INSERT, DELETE, and UPDATE are used to change the data in the database. The syntax is shown in chapter 4 and examples are shown in chapter 8.

Queries To retrieve data from the database you must use a *query*. Queries always begin with the reserved word SELECT, followed by the desired information (the target list), and the names of the tables or views containing it. Queries do not change the data. Examples of queries occur principally in chapter 8.

Data Control Statements (DCS) The Data Control Statements (DCS), such as GRANT CONNECT, REVOKE, COMMIT, ROLLBACK, LOCK TABLE, and AUDIT, control access to the data and the database, and determine how, when, and by whom data manipulations can occur. Primary examples using Data Control Statements are shown in chapter 9.

SQL datatypes

SQL in ORACLE supports the data types shown in Table 3-1. In addition to ORACLE datatypes, ORACLE SQL commands such as:

```
CREATE TABLE ...
CREATE CLUSTER ...
```

will also accept datatypes from IBM's products SQL/DS and DB2, and will internally convert them to ORACLE datatypes as shown in Table 3-2.

Table 3-3 shows all SQL commands and gives a brief description of each. The use of these commands is explained principally in chapters 7, 8, and 9.

SQL*Plus

SQL*Plus is an interface developed by Oracle Corporation for working with the ORACLE RDBMS. With it you can:

Table 3-1 ORACLE SQL Datatypes.

Name	Description
CHAR	Columns may contain alphabetic characters, digits, and all special characters. CHAR data are stored in variable length strings of ASCII or EBCDIC values. Length of a CHAR column is specified at table creation; maximum = 255.
VARCHAR	Same as CHAR. Definition might change in future versions of ORACLE.
DATE	Date fields may contain only valid dates from January 1, 4712 B.C. to December 31, 4712 A.D. When you display a date field, it appears in the standard format of DD-MON-YY.
LONG	The long datatype has more than 255 characters. It is a special variant of CHAR. A column with LONG datatype can store variable length character strings up to 65,535 characters. You are limited to one long datatype per table.
NUMBER	NUMBER columns may contain only the digits 0 through 9, and an optional negative sign. You have the option of specifying a maximum width and number of decimal places for a number field by using NUMBER (w,d) where w is the width and d is the number of decimal places.
RAW or LONG RAW	Used for byte-oriented data to be uninterpreted by ORACLE. RAW is similar to CHAR data and LONG RAW is like LONG except that no assumptions are made about the meaning of the bytes. Intended for binary data or byte strings, such as storing graphics character sequences.

Table 3-2 Conversion to IBM SQL/DS and DB2.

SQL/DS datatype	ORACLE datatype
SMALLINT	NUMBER
INTEGER	NUMBER
DECIMAL (m,n)	NUMBER (m,n)
FLOAT	NUMBER
VARCHAR (n)	VARCHAR (n)
LONG VARCHAR	LONG
GRAPHIC	no corresponding datatype
VARGRAPHIC	no corresponding datatype
LONG VARGRAPHIC	no corresponding datatype

Table 3-3 ORACLE SQL Commands.

Command	Description
/* ... */	Comment within or before a SQL command.
ALTER CLUSTER	Redefines cluster storage parameters.
ALTER DATABASE	Opens/closes, mounts/dismounts, turns archiving on/off, adds/drops logfile, and renames database.
ALTER INDEX	Redefines future storage allocation for the index.
ALTER ROLLBACK SEGMENT	Redefines future storage allocation for the rollback segment.
ALTER SEQUENCE	Redefines sequence number generation.
ALTER TABLE	Adds a column to, or redefines a column in, an existing table.
ALTER TABLESPACE	Takes tablespace off/on line, sets begin/end of backup, add/renames file, alters storage.
ALTER USER	Changes user's password, default tablespace, and default temporary segment.
AUDIT	Makes ORACLE audit use of a table, view, synonym or system facility.
COMMENT	Inserts a comment about a table or column into the data dictionary.
COMMIT	Makes permanent the changes made to the database since the last COMMIT.
CREATE CLUSTER	Creates a cluster which may contain two or more tables.
CREATE DATABASE	Creates a database instance.
CREATE DATABASELINK	Creates a link to a user name in a remote database.
CREATE INDEX	Creates an index for a table.
CREATE ROLLBACK SEGMENT	Creates a rollback segment in a tablespace.
CREATE SEQUENCE	Creates a sequence suitable for generation of primary keys.
CREATE SYNONYM	Creates a synonym for a table or view name.
CREATE TABLE	Creates a table and defines its columns and other properties.
CREATE TABLESPACE	Creates area in database for storage of tables.
CREATE VIEW	Defines a view onto one or more tables and/or other views.
DELETE	Deletes rows from a table.
DROP	Deletes a cluster, index, etc. from the database.
DROP ROLLBACK SEGMENT	Drops rollback segment in a tablespace.
DROP SEQUENCE	Drops a sequence used for generation of primary key.
DROP TABLESPACE	Drops a tablespace.

Table 3-3 Continued

Command	**Description**
GRANT	Creates user IDs, assigns passwords, grants ORACLE and table and view access privileges to users.
INSERT	Adds new rows to a table or view.
LOCK TABLE	Locks a table, enabling a user to share access to it while preserving its integrity.
NOAUDIT	Partially or completely reverses the effect of a prior AUDIT command, or of auditing options in the default table; makes ORACLE stop auditing use of a table, view, synonym or system facility.
RENAME	Changes the name of a table, view or synonym.
REVOKE	Revokes database or table access privileges from users.
ROLLBACK	Undoes all changes since the beginning of the transaction.
SAVEPOINT	Sets a point to which you may rollback.
SELECT	Performs a query; selects rows and columns from one or more tables.
SET TRANSACTION READ ONLY	Starts a read-consistent transaction.
UPDATE	Changes the values of fields in a table.
VALIDATE INDEX	Checks the integrity of a table index.

- create tables in the database
- store information in the tables
- change information in the tables
- retrieve information in a form you choose
- perform calculations on information you retrieve
- combine information you retrieve in new ways
- maintain the database

The SQL*Plus command language is easy to write and read, yet powerful enough to serve the needs of highly experienced database users. The SQL*Plus program accepts SQL*Plus commands from your keyboard, executes them through ORACLE and formats the results according to your specifications. Table 3-4 contains a summary of SQL*Plus commands and their descriptions.

Like ORACLE, SQL*Plus can run on many different kinds of systems. For information specific to your host computer, see the *ORACLE Installation and User's Guide*, published by Oracle Corporation for your equipment. To start SQL*Plus, enter:

```
SQLPLUS
```

Table 3-4 SQL*PLUS Commands.

Command	Description
@	Runs a command file.
#	Ends a sequence of comment lines begun by a DOCUMENT command.
$	Executes a host operating system command line without leaving SQL*Plus. Equivalent to HOST.
/	Runs the command in the SQL buffer.
APPEND	Appends text to the end of the current line in the current buffer.
BREAK	Specifies what events will cause a break, and what action SQL is to perform at a break.
BTITLE	Makes SQL display a title at the bottom of each page of a report.
CHANGE	Changes contents of the current line of the current buffer.
CLEAR	Clears break definitions, current buffer text, column definitions, etc.
COLUMN	Specifies how a column and a column heading should be formatted in a report.
COMPUTE	Performs computations on groups of selected rows.
CONNECT	Logs you off ORACLE and back on with a specified user name.
DEFINE	Defines a user variable and assigns it a char value.
DEL	Deletes the current line of the current buffer.
DESCRIBE	Displays a brief description of a table.
DISCONNECT	Commits pending work to the database and logs you off ORACLE, but does not terminate SQL*Plus.
DOCUMENT	Begins a block of documentation in a command file. (Not valid in programs.)
EDIT	Invokes the host system's standard text editor on the contents of the current buffer or a file.
EXIT	Terminates SQL*Plus and returns control to the operating system.
GET	Loads file into the current buffer.
HELP	Displays information about a SQL or SQL*Plus command.
HOST	Executes a host operating system command line without leaving SQL. Equivalent to "S."
INPUT	Adds new lines after the current line in the current buffer.
LIST	Lists lines of the current buffer.
NEWPAGE	Advances spooled output to the beginning of the next page. An obsolete command.
PAUSE	Displays a message, then waits for you to press the Return key.
QUIT	Terminates SQL*Plus and returns control to the operating system. A synonym for EXIT.
REMARK	Begins a remark in the program.
ROLLBACK	Rolls back (discards) changes made to the default database since changes were last committed.
RUN	Displays and runs the command in the SQL buffer.

Table 3-4 Continued

Command	Description
SAVE	Saves the contents of the current buffer (a program or SQL command) in the database or in an operating system file.
SET	Sets a system variable to a specified value.
SHOW	Displays the setting of a system variable or of a SQL*Plus property such as the current release number.
SPOOL	Manages spooling (copying) of displayed output to a system file and system printer.
SQLPLUS	System command. Starts SQL*Plus.
START	Executes the contents of a command file.
TIMING	Does performance analysis on SQL commands and SQL*Plus programs.
TTITLE	Makes SQL display a title at the top of each page of output.
UNDEFINE	Deletes the definition of a user variable.

beside your operating system prompt, and press Return. SQL*Plus will then prompt you for your user name and password. The SQL*Plus prompt will then appear:

```
SQL>
```

SQL*Plus will accept both SQL and SQL*Plus commands.

SQL command syntax in SQL*Plus

All SQL commands must end with a semicolon (;). You may enter your command on a single line, or on as many lines as you wish as long as individual words are not broken up between one line and the next. If your command is longer than one line, SQL*Plus will prompt you for the next line by entering a 2 (for line two), then a 3 (for line three), etc., until you conclude the command with a semicolon.

Words in a SQL command must be separated by at least one space. Whether or not you use upper- or lowercase in making up your SQL command is sometimes significant in SQL*Plus. Case will make a difference when you enter a:

- *CHAR value* A CHAR value is a sequence of characters that SQL*Plus is to process. If you enter a command telling SQL*Plus to display the CHAR value "Annual Report" as a heading, this is different from "ANNUAL REPORT" and from "annual report." Therefore, in expressing the CHAR value, you must use upper- and lowercase in exactly the form in which you want it to appear.
- *user name* "MARY," "Mary," and "mary" are three different user names. The same is true for passwords: Uppercase is not exchangeable with lowercase for a user name or password.

Case will not make any difference when you enter the name of a:

- *table, column or other object in the database* "EMPLOYEE," "Employee," and "employee" are all the same table in the database.
- *reserved word* Reserved words such as SELECT and FROM can be written in any combination of upper- and lowercase letters, such as "SELECT," "Select" or "select." (The list of SQL reserved words appears in Table 4-1 in chapter 4.)

SQL*Plus command syntax

SQL*Plus command syntax is slightly different from SQL command syntax. Usually a SQL*Plus command is entered on a single line. However, if you reach the end of the line without finishing the command, you may continue on the next line but do not press Return. Instead, enter a hyphen (-) at the end of every line except the last. You should only press the Return when you have finished the entire command no matter how many lines it takes. But you must enter a hyphen at the end of every line that is not the end of the command.

You don't have to end a SQL*Plus command with a semicolon although you may put one there if you wish. But you must end a SQL*Plus command with a Return.

Editing SQL commands with SQL*Plus

Some editing commands are listed in Table 3-5 that can be used to examine, change or rerun a SQL command without re-entering it.

Table 3-5 SQL*PLUS Editing Commands.

Command	Abbreviation	Purpose
APPEND text	A text	Add text at the end of a line
CHANGE	C/old/new/	Change old text to new in a line
CHANGE	C/text/	Delete text from a line
CLEAR BUFFER	CL BUFF	Delete all lines
DEL	(none)	Delete a line
INPUT	I	Add an indefinite number of lines
INPUT	Itext	Add a line consisting of text
LIST	L	List all lines in the SQL buffer
LIST n	L n	List a specified line
LIST m n	L m n	List lines from m to n
RUN	R	Rerun the current SQL command
SAVE	SAV	Save contents of current buffer into a host system file.

Correcting a mistake

If you make a mistake in entering a command, use the Backspace key to erase it, and enter it over again. However, if you have already pressed Return, the Backspace key will not remove an error. In that case, if the mistake was in a SQL command, use the editing commands shown in Table 3-4. If the mistake was in a SQL*Plus command, re-enter the command correctly.

The editing commands are especially useful in correcting typing errors or in modifying a query you have entered. When you enter a SQL command, SQL*Plus stores it in the buffer, and it stays there until you enter another command. This stored command is called the "current SQL command."

All of the editing commands except LIST and RUN affect a line in the buffer. This line is called the "current line," and is marked with an asterisk when the current command is listed.

For example, if you want to display the contents of the SQL buffer, enter:

```
LIST
```

beside the SQL prompt (SQL>).

SQL*Plus will then return the following (in which the SQL*Plus prompt numbers are shown so that we can exhibit the asterisk beside the line number).

```
1 SELECT *
2 FROM EMPLOYEES
3* WHERE SALESMAN = 432
```

The asterisk after line number three means that line three is the current line. If you enter a CHANGE command at this point, the change will affect that line.

Any semicolons that you enter at the end of the original command are not listed when SQL*Plus displays the contents of the buffer because the semicolon is not stored (even though you must use it in a SQL command when you enter the command). The LIST command does not need a semicolon when you enter it because it is a SQL*Plus command rather than a SQL command.

If you make a mistake, for example, in entering a column name, you will get an error message indicating the line containing the mistake. Suppose you mistakenly try to select from STRENO instead of STORENO, the error message would look like this:

```
SELECT STRENO
         *
ERROR at line 1: ORA-0704: invalid column name
```

In this message, the asterisk shows where the error is in the mistyped column name STRENO. Now, instead of retyping the entire command, you can correct the mistake by editing the command in the buffer, like this:

1. Enter LIST followed by the line number to display the line containing the error, and make it the current line.
2. Enter the CHANGE command to correct the mistake. You will need to enter the following three items separated by slashes:
   - The word CHANGE (or the letter C)
   - The sequence of characters containing the error
   - The sequence of characters you want to insert to make the change.

To change STRENO to STORENO, edit the misspelled column this way (SQL*Plus prompts are shown at the left to make the process clear):

1. Enter LIST and the line number you want to change:

   ```
   SQL> LIST 1
   ```

2. When the following line appears on the screen:

   ```
   1* SELECT STRENO
   ```

   enter this:

   ```
   SQL> CHANGE /STRENO/STORENO/
   ```

   and the corrected line will appear:

   ```
   1* SELECT STORENO
   ```

The CHANGE command will find the first occurrence of the designated character sequence in the current line and will change it to the new sequence. After changing a command, you can use the RUN command to put it on the screen again. Just enter

```
RUN
```

and the complete, corrected command will be shown on your screen and executed.

Inserting a new line

To add a new line to the buffer or to insert a line between existing lines, use the INPUT command. After doing so, you might want to again use the RUN command to see and execute the revised version of the original command.

Appending text to a line

If you want to add text to the end of a line in the buffer, use the APPEND command as follows:

1. Display the line you want to change with the LIST command.
2. Enter APPEND followed by the text you want to add.

If the text you are adding begins with a blank, separate the word APPEND from the first character of the text by two blanks—one to separate the command from the text, and one to go into the buffer with the text.

Deleting a line

Use the DEL command to delete a line in the buffer.

1. Display the line you want to delete with the LIST command.
2. Enter DEL.

This makes the following line of the buffer, if any, the current line. You can delete several consecutive lines, by making the first of them the current line, then deleting each one consecutively.

Storing and printing results

You might want to store the results of a query in a file so that you can edit them with a word processor before printing them, or including them in some other document. To store them in a file and also display them on the screen, enter:

```
SPOOL <file>.LIS
```

All information displayed on the screen after you enter this command will be stored in the file you specified before .LIS. The .LIS identifies this file as a listing file. However, if there is already a period (.) in the file name you specify in the SPOOL command, you cannot use the .LIS suffix.

SQL*Plus will continue to spool information to the file you designated until you stop it by entering:

```
SPOOL OFF
```

To print query results instead of just stopping the spooling, instead of SPOOL OFF, enter:

```
SPOOL OUT
```

SQL*Plus will stop spooling and will copy the spool file's contents to your host computer's printer.

Help messages

SQL*Plus has a great many help panels showing available commands and how to use them. For a display of all SQL and SQL*Plus commands, just enter:

```
HELP
```

For a display about a specific command, enter the word HELP followed by the name of the command, as follows:

```
HELP SELECT
```

Error messages

If SQL*Plus detects an error in a command, it will display an error message. Often, you will be able to detect the error from the content of the message and correct it. If not, look the message up in ORACLE Corporation's publication *Error Messages and Codes* to find the cause of the problem and how to correct it.

Interrupting the display

If you want SQL*Plus to pause after each screen of a long report is displayed, you may use the SET PAUSE command. Enter:

```
SET PAUSE ON <text>
```

and fill in the text you want displayed before the pause. After each pause, SQL*Plus will wait for you to press Return before continuing to scroll. To get rid of this pause, enter:

```
SET PAUSE OFF
```

and press Return.

Stopping the display

To stop a multi-page display before it comes to the end, press the Interrupt (or Break) key. This key is operating-system specific; in most systems you can accomplish an interrupt by pressing Ctrl-C (^C). SQL*Plus will then stop the display and return to the prompt. However, pressing the Interrupt key will not stop a parsing operation once it is in progress.

Leaving SQL*Plus

When you are done working with SQL*Plus and wish to return to the operating system, enter the following:

```
EXIT
```

Running other programs

You can execute a host operating system command while you are in SQL*Plus, as for example, if you want to look at the contents of the host operating system directory. To do this, enter the SQL*Plus command HOST followed by the host command. For example, on DEC VMS, enter the following:

```
HOST DIR *.SQL;
```

When the host command has finished running, the SQL*Plus prompt will reappear.

Executing a command from a file

To retrieve a query from a file and run it in a single step, use the START command, followed by the name of the file:

```
START <filename>
```

You don't need to add the .SQL suffix in this case.

Including SQL*Plus commands in a command file

When you store the current SQL command in a file using the SAVE command, the SQL*Plus commands you entered do not get stored with it. When you retrieve this command file later, you will have to re-enter the SQL*Plus commands if you want the same result.

To store the SQL*Plus command file along with the SQL commands, use the SET command to set up a current buffer that is not the SQL buffer. The command to do this is:

```
SET BUFFER <name>
```

where name is any word that obeys the usual rules for naming a SQL*Plus object. Now all edit commands will operate on the new current buffer instead of the SQL buffer.

Now use the SQL*Plus editor to place your SQL*Plus commands and the SQL command together in your new current buffer. Save the commands with SAVE, and run them with START.

EDIT command: Using the host system's text editor

If you wish to use your host system's text editor rather than the SQL*Plus editing commands, you can do so by entering:

```
EDIT
```

which will edit the contents of the current buffer. If you tell the text editor to save edited text, that text will be saved back into the current buffer. Or, you may edit the contents of a specific file by entering:

```
EDIT <filename>
```

A .SQL file suffix will be assumed for the file. If this is not the suffix you want, you must state your file suffix on the EDIT command line. If you save the command file with the text editor, it will be saved back into the same file.

Using SQL and SQL*Plus

Details of using SQL and SQL*Plus for creating database objects, and for querying and maintaining the database are in chapters 7, 8, and 9.

Summary

This chapter introduces SQL, the Structured Query Language, and ORACLE's user-friendly interface, SQL*Plus, and gives general instructions for their use in the ORACLE RDBMS.

4
CHAPTER

Components of SQL in ORACLE

Although SQL is described as a "query language," it is actually much more than that because it contains many other capabilities besides querying a database. These include features for: (1) defining the structure of the data, (2) modifying data in the database, and (3) specifying security constraints. Each feature has its own set of statements that are expressed in the Data Definition Language (DDL), Data Manipulation Language (DML), and Data Control Language (DCL), respectively. An overview showing the syntax of these three features is presented in this chapter. Further details of their many uses appear in chapter 7 and succeeding chapters.

SQL in ORACLE also contains sets of words and symbols used in specifying the results of commands. These are called *value expressions*, *logical connectives*, *predicates*, *table expressions*, *SQL functions*, and *subqueries*. The syntax for each of these is exhibited in the sections that follow. In each case, examples showing how these are used in a sample database, appear in later chapters.

The catalog

The *catalog* is a system database containing information about base tables, views, access rights, user-IDs, etc., that can be queried through the use of SQL SELECT statements.

In the ORACLE RDBMS, the catalog contains tables of such information, just like the tables containing the database that is stored and accessed by the user. Its purpose is to provide the user with information about the contents of the database. You cannot apply the UPDATE, INSERT INTO or DELETE commands to the catalog because the operation of the database is dependent on it and any change made by a user could destroy the integrity of the database.

SQL commands

The SQL language consists of a set of commands together with rules for using them. Table 3-3 in chapter 3 gives the basic ORACLE SQL commands along with a brief description of each.

Reserved words

The words forming the SQL commands, as well as the qualifying words used with them, are all designated as reserved words. You may not use these words as names of tables, views or columns without applying special symbols to them that will distinguish them from their reserved word function. Table 4-1 lists the ORACLE SQL reserved words.

Table 4-1 ORACLE SQL Reserved Words.

ACCESS, ADD, ALL, ALTER, AND, ANY, AS, ASC, AUDIT

BETWEEN, BY

CHAR, CHECK, CLUSTER, COLUMN, COMMENT, COMPRESS, CONNECT, CREATE,

CURRENT

DATE, DBA, DECIMAL, DEFAULT, DELETE, DESC, DISTINCT, DROP

ELSE, EXCLUSIVE, EXISTS

FILE, FLOAT, FOR, FROM

GRANT, GRAPHIC, GROUP

HAVING

IDENTIFIED, IF, IMMEDIATE, IN, INCREMENT, INDEX, INITIAL, INSERT,

INTEGER, INTERSECT, INTO, IS

LEVEL, LIKE, LOCK, LONG

Table 4-1 Continued

MAXETENTS, MINUS, MODE, MODIFY
NOAUDIT, NOCOMPRESS, NOT, NOWAIT, NULL, NUMBER
OF, OFFLINE, ON, ONLINE, OPTION, OR, ORDER
PCTFREE, PRIOR, PRIVILEGES, PUBLIC
RAW, RENAME, RESOURCE, REVOKE, ROW, ROWID, ROWNUM, ROWS
SELECT, SESSION, SET, SHARE, SIZE, SMALLINT, START, SUCCESSFUL,
SYNONYM, SYSDATE
TABLE, THEN, TO, TRIGGER
UID, UNION, UNIQUE, UPDATE, USER
VALIDATE, VALUES, VARCHAR, VARGRAPHIC, VIEW
WHENEVER, WHERE, WITH

Datatypes

ORACLE SQL supports six major datatypes: Character (CHAR), VARCHAR, DATE, LONG, NUMBER, RAW or LONG RAW. You can do arithmetic with the values in NUMBER and DATE columns. Descriptions of the datatypes supported by SQL in ORACLE appear in Table 3-1 in chapter 3.

Some datatypes are case sensitive (will distinguish between upper- and lowercase letters) and some are not. As situations arise, we will point out when it is important to capitalize, and when it is not necessary.

Value expressions

SQL in ORACLE supports these value expressions:

addition (+)
subtraction (−)
multiplication (*)
division (/)

The use of these expressions will be illustrated in connection with other expressions, functions, and operators in the sections and chapters that follow.

Logical connectives

SQL in ORACLE provides for the logical connectives, AND, OR, and NOT and also for what are usually called the Boolean operators, INTERSECT, UNION, and MINUS. These are all discussed in chapter 6.

Predicates

A *predicate* is a condition that can be evaluated to produce a truth value of "true," "false" or "unknown." This result is achieved by applying the predicate to a given row of a table. The predicates, also called *comparison operators*, supported by ORACLE SQL are:

comparison (=, <>, <, >, <=, =>)
between (...BETWEEN ... AND ...)
IN, (NOT IN)
LIKE
IS NULL, IS NOT NULL
quantified (ALL, SOME, ANY)
EXISTS, NOT EXISTS

These predicates are discussed and illustrated in chapter 5.

The Data Definition Language (DDL)

A database scheme must be specified by a set of definitions. These can be expressed in the SQL Data Definition Language (DDL), which consists of the Data Definition Statements (DDS) CREATE DATABASE, CREATE TABLESPACE, CREATE TABLE, CREATE CLUSTER, CREATE INDEX, CREATE SEQUENCE, CREATE SYNONYM, CREATE ROLLBACK SEGMENT, CREATE DATABASE LINK, ALTER TABLE, ALTER CLUSTER, ALTER DATABASE, ALTER INDEX, ALTER SEQUENCE, ALTER TABLESPACE, ALTER USER, DROP CLUSTER, DROP DATABASE LINK, DROP SEQUENCE, DROP SYNONYM, DROP TABLE, DROP TABLESPACE, DROP VIEW, and DROP INDEX.

When the DDSs are completed with the appropriate clauses and predicates, and executed, the result is a set of tables and indices. The names of these are then stored in the catalog tables. The syntax of each of the DDL statements is shown in the sections that follow.

CREATE DATABASE

You must start by creating the database by using the CREATE DATABASE command. This will create new database files; write the initial database data that ORACLE requires for normal operation; and create and initialize the control and redo log files.

You only need to create the database once, regardless of its size. If you use the CREATE DATABASE command on an existing database, you will lose all data in the original database.

Only a database administrator (DBA) can create a database. There are several steps to be performed in starting a database in addition to the CRE-

ATE DATABASE command; these are mentioned in chapter 7. The syntax for creating a database is:

```
CREATE DATABASE <database_name>
[CONTROLFILE REUSE]
[LOGFILE <filespec> [,<filespec>] ...]
[MAXLOGFILES <integer> ]
[DATAFILE <filespec> [,<filespec> ] ... ]
[MAXDATAFILES <integer> ]
[MAXINSTANCES <integer> ]
[ARCHIVELOG/NOARCHIVELOG]
[SHARED/EXCLUSIVE];
```

where:

<database>	is the name of the database, which can be a maximum of eight characters.
<filespec>	is the specification of a database file in the form: SIZE <integer> [K|M]] REUSE, where <integer> specifies a size in number of bytes. No <integer> means ORACLE will use the default size of 10M for database files or the default size of 500K for log files. If <integer> is followed by K, then SIZE is computed as the <integer> multiplied by 1024. If M is used, then SIZE will be the <integer> multiplied by 1048576.
CONTROLFILE REUSE	specifies that existing control files identified by the INIT.ORA parameter, CONTROL_FILES should be reused, thus ignoring and overwriting any information they may currently contain.
LOGFILE	specifies one or more files to be used as redo log files. Default is two redo log files.
MAXLOGFILES	specifies maximum number of redo log files that can ever be created for this database. Sets the absolute limit. The valid range is 2–256.
DATAFILE	specifies one or more files to be used for database files. Default is one.
MAXDATAFILES	specifies the maximum number of database files that can ever be created for this database. Valid range is O/S dependent, usually 1–255. Default is 32.

MAXINSTANCES	specifies the maximum number of instances that can ever simultaneously mount and open this database. The valid range is 1–255.
ARCHIVELOG/ NOARCHIVELOG	specifies the initial mode of using redo log files. Mode can be changed with the ALTER DATABASE statement. Default is NOARCHIVELOG, indicating that a redo log file can be reused without archiving its contents.
SHARED/ EXCLUSIVE	specifies how the database should be left mounted after it is created. Applies only to this startup; after initial database creation this choice is made via the STARTUP statement by each instance opening a database. SHARED indicates that multiple instances may access this database. EXCLUSIVE indicates that only one instance may access it.

Note that all of the arguments are optional except the database name.

CREATE TABLESPACE

The tablespace is the primary logical division of a database. You will use it for space allocation, online availability, and recovery. You need DBA privileges (see Data Control Language in a later section of this chapter) to create, alter or drop a tablespace.

The syntax for creating a tablespace is as follows:

```
CREATE TABLESPACE <tablespace>
DATAFILE <filespec> [,<filespec>] ...
[DEFAULT STORAGE (
    [INITIAL <n>] [NEXT <n>]
    [MINEXTENTS <n>] [MAXEXTENTS {<n>/NULL}]
    [PCTINCREASE <n>])
    [ONLINE/OFFLINE]];
```

CREATE TABLE

The DDL statement to create a table must contain the column names, their datatypes, and the sizes of the data to be entered. The syntax is as follows:

```
CREATE TABLE        <tablename>
(<column1_name>     <datatype>(<datasize>),
```

```
<column2_name>      <datatype>(<datasize>),
...
<columnN_name>      <datatype>(<datasize>));
```

Note that the entire description of the columns is enclosed in parentheses. Information about consecutive columns must be separated by commas.

When you create a table in ORACLE, the table name

- can be up to 30 characters long.
- must begin with one of the letters from A through Z.
- after the initial letter, may contain any letter from A through Z, any number from 0 through 9, and any of the four symbols _, #, $, @. (But see the exception at the end of this list.)
- is the same whether upper- or lowercase letters are used, for example EMPLOYEES, Employees, and employees are all the same table name as far as ORACLE is concerned. (But see the exception at the end of this list.)
- cannot have the same name as another table or view. (Views are discussed in the section on the Data Manipulation Language.)
- cannot duplicate an ORACLE or SQL reserved word. ORACLE SQL reserved words appear in Table 4-1.
- if enclosed in apostrophes when created, can contain any combination of characters, except an apostrophe in the name itself.
- if enclosed in apostrophes when created, will return the name exactly as entered with regard to upper- or lowercase, for example 'EMPLOYEES,' 'Employees,' and 'employees' are not the same table, they are three different tables.

Column names follow the same rules as those shown for table names. Keep in mind that if you do not specify a column width, ORACLE will ask for a width. (Check the documentation for the machine you are using to determine the maximum number of columns possible.) And as with a table name, each column name in a specified table must be unique. In other words, no table can contain more than one column with the same name.

Specify NOT NULL if your operation requires that the data for a certain column is essential. Then if anyone tries to enter a record without filling in a value for that column, ORACLE will return an error message.

Inserting rows of data values in a table requires one or more of the Data Manipulation Statements discussed later in this chapter, or you will need to import data via the SQL*Loader, an ORACLE utility. See chapter 7 for further details of the CREATE TABLE command, as well as illustrations of its use.

CREATE CLUSTER

Clustering can improve the performance of your system by letting several related tables share the same extents of disk space. In particular, it can improve the performance of join queries because rows that are joined are stored together.

First you create a cluster, then you create the tables and specify that they are to be in the cluster. The syntax for creating the cluster itself is:

```
CREATE CLUSTER <cluster>
(<column spec> <, column spec> , ... );
```

where:

<cluster>	is the name of the cluster.
<column spec>	is the size and width of a named column.

CREATE INDEX

To create an index on a specified table, the SQL command is:

```
CREATE INDEX <indexname>
    ON <tablename> (<column_name>);
```

You can create as many indices as you wish on any one table. You can have an index for each column in the table, as well as an index for a combination of columns. How many and what type of indices you create for a given table will depend on the type of queries you expect will be directed to the database, and the size of the database. Too many indices can be as great a liability as too few. More on this in chapter 11.

The only operations that you can perform directly on indices are CREATE and DROP. SQL Data Manipulation Statements such as SELECT cannot be implemented by any user for an index because, in order to optimize retrieval, decisions about which index to use in answering a SQL query are made by the system. (See chapter 11, however, for ways to influence ORACLE's use of indices by strategic placement of expressions within a query.)

CREATE SEQUENCE

You can use sequence numbers independently of transactions to automatically generate unique primary keys for your data and to coordinate the keys across multiple rows or tables. The syntax is:

```
CREATE SEQUENCE <sequence_name>
    [INCREMENT BY {1/<n>}]
    [START WITH <n>]
    [MAXVALUE <n>] / [NOMAXVALUE]
    [MINVALUE <n>] / [NOMINVALUE]
    [CYCLE] / [NOCYCLE]
```

```
[CACHE <n>] / [NOCACHE]
[ORDER] / [NOORDER];
```

where:

sequence_name	is the name you give the sequence, and is subject to the same naming rules as other database objects.
INCREMENT BY	determines the interval between sequence numbers. If negative, then the sequence will descend; if positive, the sequence will ascend. Default is 1 ascending.
START WITH	is the first sequence number created. The default is MINVALUE for ascending sequences, MAXVALUE for descending sequences.
MINVALUE/ NOMINVALUE	sets the minimum value to be generated. For ascending, the default is MINVALUE with a value of 1. For descending, default is NOMINVALUE.
MAXVALUE/ NOMAXVALUE	sets maximum value to be generated. Default is NOMAXVALUE. For descending, default is MAXVALUE with a value of –1.
CYCLE/NOCYCLE	The default is NOCYCLE. A sequence will either grow without bounds, stop at a predefined limit, or restart after reaching the limit. For a sequence to grow without bounds, do not specify a MAX VALUE for ascending sequences or a MINVALUE for descending sequences. For a sequence that stops at a limit, specify a MAXVALUE for ascending or a MINVALUE for descending and specify NOCYCLE. For a sequence that restarts after reaching a limit, specify a MAXVALUE for an ascending sequence limit or a MINVALUE for a descending sequence limit, and specify CYCLE.
CACHE/NOCACHE	will pre-allocate sequence numbers so they can be kept in memory, resulting in faster generation of numbers. Use for applications with high performance requirements. NOCACHE is the default.
ORDER/NOORDER	specifies that sequence numbers are guaranteed to be generated in order of request. Important for applications that use sequence numbers as timestamps. Usually not important for tables using sequences to generate primary keys.

Sequence numbers are used with the two words NEXTVAL and CURRVAL, which are not reserved words, and can therefore be used as pseudo-column names in SQL statements.

CREATE SYNONYM

CREATE SYNONYM creates a synonym for a table name or view name. You must own the table or have a SELECT privilege on it to create a synonym. The syntax is:

```
CREATE [PUBLIC] SYNONYM <synonym_name>
FOR [<user.>] <table> [<databaselink>];
```

where:

<synonym_name>	is the name you give the synonym and is subject to the naming rules for other database objects.
<user>	is an existing user name in the database. If you omit user, the command assumes you own the table or view.
PUBLIC	indicates that you are creating a synonym that any user can refer to without qualification. If omitted, users other than yourself must qualify the synonym with your user name. Only a DBA can create a PUBLIC synonym.
<table>	is an existing table in the database.
<databaselink>	is an existing link to a remote database.

CREATE DATABASE LINK

Suppose you have SQL*Net installed on your local database and on a remote database. If you have access to an ORACLE user name on the remote database, you can create a link from your local database to that remote user name. However, only a DBA can create public database links. The syntax is:

```
CREATE [PUBLIC] DATABASE LINK <link>
CONNECT TO <user> [IDENTIFIED BY <password>]
USING <'SQL*NET_string'>;
```

where:

<link>	is the name to be given to the database link.
<user>	is a valid user name on the specified remote database.
<password>	is a valid password for the specified user on the remote database.

SQL*Net_string — is the database specification of a remote database accessible through SQL*Net. This information is available to the DBA.

When the PUBLIC option is omitted, the link is available only to its creator. Remote tables are referenced in queries by adding @<linkname> to remote tables in the FROM clause of the SELECT statement.

ALTER CLUSTER

If you want to redefine future storage parameters for a cluster, use the SQL command ALTER CLUSTER. You cannot change the columns that make up the cluster key, nor does the ALTER CLUSTER command change the cluster's tablespace. The syntax is:

```
ALTER CLUSTER [<user.>] <cluster>
    [PCTUSED <n>] [PCTFREE <n>]
    [SIZE <n>]
    [INITRANS <n>] [MAXTRANS <n>]
    [STORAGE <storage>];
```

You will find more information on clusters in chapter 7.

ALTER DATABASE

You can use the ALTER DATABASE command to mount a database; open or close a database; add or drop a redo log file; rename a redo log file or database file; or specify that the redo log will or will not be archived. Only a DBA can alter a database. The database does not need to be currently mounted or open when you alter it. The syntax is:

```
ALTER DATABASE [<database>]
[ADD LOGFILE <filespec> [, <filespec>] ...]
    [DROP LOGFILE <text> [,<text>] ...]
    [RENAME FILE <text> [,<text>] ... TO <text> [,<text>] ...]
    [ARCHIVELOG / NOARCHIVELOG]
    [MOUNT [SHARED / EXCLUSIVE] / DISMOUNT]
    [OPEN / CLOSE [NORMAL / IMMEDIATE ]];
```

where:

<database> — is a name for the database, which cannot exceed eight characters. If omitted, the default value for the parameter DB_Name in the current INIT.ORA file is assumed.

ADD LOGFILE <filespec> — is a specification of a database file in the form:

	'filename' [SIZE <integer>[K|M]] where <integer> specifies a size in a number of bytes. No <integer> means ORACLE will use the default logfile size of 500K. If the <integer> is followed by K, then SIZE is computed as the <integer> multiplied by 1024. If M is used, then SIZE will be the <integer> multiplied by 1048576.
DROP LOGFILE <filename>	is the name of a current redo log file to be dropped.
RENAME FILE <filename> to <filename>	specifies old and new file names for database files. New file names must adhere to your standard operating system file name conventions.
ARCHIVELOG/ NOARCHIVELOG	enables and disables archiving, respectively.
MOUNT/DISMOUNT	permits/disallows DBA-only functions.
OPEN/CLOSE	permits/disallows standard user access to the database.

ALTER INDEX

You can use the ALTER INDEX command to change future storage allocation for index blocks. To do so, you must be the owner of the index or have DBA privileges. The syntax is:

```
ALTER INDEX [ <user>.] <index>
    [INITRANS <n>] [MAXTRANS <n>]
    [STORAGE <storage>];
```

where:

<index>	is the index name
<storage>	is the same as in ALTER TABLESPACE

ALTER ROLLBACK SEGMENT

You can alter an existing rollback segment by making it public, or by altering the storage parameters. You can only use this command if you are the DBA. The syntax is:

```
ALTER [PUBLIC] ROLLBACK SEGMENT &lt;segment&gt;
    STORAGE <storage>;
```

where:

PUBLIC	if specified, indicates that the rollback segment should become a public one, available for use by any instance. If omitted, indicates that the rollback segment should not be a public one.
<segment>	specifies an existing rollback segment.
STORAGE <storage>	specifies the characteristics of database storage for the rollback segment.

ALTER SEQUENCE

You can use the ALTER SEQUENCE command to change any of the options you used when you created the sequence, except the starting value. If you want to start the sequence at a different number, you must drop the sequence and create it again.

In altering the sequence, you cannot impose a new MAXVALUE that is less than the old MAXVALUE or lower than the current sequence number. The syntax is:

```
ALTER SEQUENCE <sequence>
    [INCREMENT BY { I/<n> }]
    [MAXVALUE <n>] / [NOMAXVALUE]
    [MINVALUE <n>] / [NOMINVALUE]
    [CYCLE] / [NOCYCLE]
    [CACHE <n>] / [NOCACHE]
    [ORDER] / [NOORDER];
```

where the meaning of the arguments shown is the same as in the CREATE SEQUENCE statement.

ALTER TABLE

As new situations develop, or new data are presented for the database to store, the original definition of a table might no longer suffice. You can alter an existing base table at any time by adding table elements, modifying column definitions, dropping constraints, or modifying future storage allocations. The complete syntax is:

```
ALTER TABLE [<user.>] <tablename>
[ADD {<table_element>/(<table_element> [,<table_element>] ...)}]
[MODIFY {<column_def>/(<column_def> [,<column_def>] ...)}]
[DROP CONSTRAINT {<constraint>/ [,<constraint>] ...)}]
[PCTFREE <integer>] [PCTUSED <integer>]
[INITRANS <integer>] [MAXTRANS <integer>]
```

```
[STORAGE <storage>]
[BACKUP];
```

where:

<user>	is the owner of the table.
<tablename>	is the name of an existing table that you own or have the privilege to alter.
<table-element>	is a well-defined, unique column heading.
<column definition>	is a column specification in the table represented by the <tablename>.
<constraints>	are restrictions on columns in the table, such as NOT NULL or UNIQUE.
<storage>	defines future space allocation.
PCTFREE and PCTUSED	determine whether inserted rows will go into existing blocks or new blocks. PCTFREE ranges from 0 to 100, and is the percent of the table that will not be filled with inserted rows. Rows are stored in ORACLE blocks, with block size o/s dependent, usually from 1024 to 4096 bytes. A value of 0 for PCTFREE means that the block will be filled. PCTFREE defaults to 10.
BACKUP	updates the data dictionary to indicate that the table has been backed up as of the time of the ALTER TABLE statement.

You also can use the ALTER command to modify the columns within a table by increasing a column width or changing the number of decimal places. You may decrease a column's width, or change its datatype only if all values in the column are NULL. Examples of the use of the ALTER TABLE command to modify column specifications appear in chapter 7.

ALTER TABLESPACE

You can alter a tablespace by adding or renaming a database file(s), changing default storage parameters, taking the tablespace online or offline, and starting or stopping backup. You must have DBA privileges to alter a tablespace. The syntax is:

```
ALTER TABLESPACE <tablespace>
[ADD DATAFILE <filespec> [,<filespec>] ... ]
[RENAME DATAFILE <text> [,<text>] ... TO <text> [, <text>] ... ]
[DEFAULT STORAGE <storage>]
[ONLINE/OFFLINE [NORMAL/IMMEDIATE]]
[BEGIN BACKUP/ END BACKUP];
```

where:

<tablespace>	is the name of an existing tablespace
<filespec>	is a specification of a database file in the form <'filename'> [SIZE <integer> [K/M]] [REUSE] where integer specifies a size in number of bytes. No integer means that ORACLE will use the default tablespace size of 10M. If the integer is followed by K, then SIZE is the integer multiplied by 1024. If M is used, then SIZE will be the integer multiplied by 1048576.
<text>	is either the old or new file name (enclosed in single quotes).
<storage>	allows you to specify the following: [INITIAL <integer>] [NEXT <integer>] [MINEXTENTS <integer>] [MAXEXTENTS <integer>] [PCTINCREASE <pct>]
ONLINE	means that the tablespace is to be brought back online.
OFFLINE	means that the tablespace is to be taken offline either immediately or after all current users finish accessing it.
BEGIN BACKUP	means that the database files making up this tablespace are undergoing a system backup procedure. Has no effect on access. Useful mostly for the control file and redo log record-keeping.

ALTER USER

You can use the ALTER USER command to alter passwords, default tablespaces for object creation, and default temporary tablespaces for temporary segments created on behalf of the user. (You also can change a user's password with the GRANT command.) You must have DBA privilege to use the ALTER USER command. The syntax is:

```
ALTER USER <user>
    [IDENTIFIED BY <password>]
    [DEFAULT TABLESPACE <tablespace>]
    [TEMPORARY TABLESPACE <tablespace>];
```

where:

<username>	is the currently valid user name for a database user.

<password>	is the new password for the specified user.
DEFAULT TABLESPACE	specifies the default tablespace for object creation.
TEMPORARY TABLESPACE	specifies the default temporary tablespace for the creation of temporary segments.

DROP CLUSTER

You can drop a cluster if you own it or if you are the DBA. The syntax is:

```
DROP CLUSTER [<user>.] <cluster> [INCLUDING TABLES];
```

where:

<user>	is the owner of the cluster.
<cluster>	is the name of an existing cluster.
INCLUDING TABLES	drops all the tables that belong to the cluster. If not specified, the cluster must be empty to be dropped.

DROP DATABASE LINK

You can drop a database link that you own. The syntax is:

```
DROP [PUBLIC] DATABASE LINK <databaselink>;
```

Only the DBA can use the option of dropping a public database link.

DROP INDEX

To drop an index, use the SQL DROP command followed by the name of the index:

```
DROP INDEX <index_name>
    ON <tablename>;
```

If you have indices with the same name defined on different tables, the ON <tablename> command must be used, as shown in the syntax, to distinguish the index you want to drop.

If there is no other index with that name on any other table, then you don't need to specify the table name. The following DROP command will be sufficient:

```
DROP INDEX <index_name>;
```

When you drop an index, this does not drop the tables or views on which the index is based.

DROP SEQUENCE

You can drop any sequence that you own, or if you are the DBA. The syntax is:

```
DROP SEQUENCE [<user>.] <sequence>;
```

where:

<user>	is the name of the owner of the sequence.
<sequence>	is the name of the sequence.

DROP TABLE

To drop a table, you must be the DBA or own the table. The syntax is:

```
DROP TABLE [user.] table;
```

If you drop a table, you also drop the indices for that table. This does not drop the views or synonyms that were created on that table, but they do become invalid. Such views and synonyms should then be dropped or redefined so that they become useful again. The DROP TABLE command returns all blocks allocated to that table to the tablespaces containing the data unless the table was a member of a cluster.

DROP TABLESPACE

Only a DBA can drop a tablespace. You cannot drop a tablespace unless it is offline. The syntax is:

```
DROP TABLESPACE <tablespace> [INCLUDING CONTENTS]
```

The Data Manipulation Language (DML)

After data are loaded into the tables created by the DDL statements of the previous section, the Data Manipulation Language (DML) will make it possible to perform manipulations on them, including inserting, updating, deleting, and querying—for example, by using the SQL SELECT statement.

Creating a view involves manipulating data in tables that are already in the database. Therefore, creating views is discussed in the context of data manipulation, rather than in the context of data definition. The syntax for the basic forms of these operations is illustrated in the sections that follow.

INSERT

The initial loading into the database of large batches of data in a general loading operation is handled by means of the ORACLE product called

SQL*Loader. The SQL INSERT statement is used to add new individual rows of data to what already exists in the database. The syntax is:

```
INSERT
INTO <tablename> (<column1_name>, <column2_name>, ...)
VALUES (<value1>, <value2>, ...);
```

If the list of values is in the same sequence as the sequence of the columns in the table, and there is a value for every column in the table, then the list of column names can be omitted. Otherwise, the column names must be specified as shown. Values inserted must match the datatype of the column into which they are being inserted. CHAR values must be enclosed in single quotes. Do not enclose either NUM values or the NULL value in quotes.

UPDATE

The UPDATE command is used to change the values in existing rows. Its general form is:

```
UPDATE    <tablename>
SET       <column1> = <newvalue1>,
          <column2> = <newvalue2>,
          ...
          <columnN> = <newvalueN>,
[WHERE    <condition>];
```

The SET clause of the UPDATE command tells which columns to update and the new values to insert.

The UPDATE command operates on all the rows that meet the condition specified by the WHERE clause. The WHERE clause is optional, but if it is omitted all rows will be updated with the new values shown in the SET clause.

You can update multiple columns in each row with a single UPDATE command by listing multiple columns after the SET clause.

The WHERE clause in an UPDATE command may contain a subquery. The use of subqueries for this and other purposes is discussed in chapter 6.

DELETE

The DELETE command is used to remove rows from a table. Its general form is:

```
DELETE
FROM      <tablename>
WHERE     <condition>;
```

You cannot delete partial rows, therefore you do not have to specify column names in the DELETE command.

The WHERE clause determines which rows will be removed. If you want to delete all rows from a table, omit the WHERE clause, and enter the command:

```
DELETE
FROM     <tablename>;
```

This will remove all rows, leaving only the column specifications and table name.

SELECT

The basic structure of a SQL query consists of the three clauses:

```
SELECT   <column1>, <column2>, ...
FROM     <tablename>
WHERE    <condition>;
```

where:

SELECT	lists the columns desired in the result of the query; these are called the *target list*. (This clause corresponds to the projection operation of relational algebra.)
FROM	names the table to be scanned in the execution of the expression.
WHERE	corresponds to the selection predicate of the relational algebra. It consists of a predicate involving columns of the table(s) that appear(s) in the FROM clause.

The SELECT command and the FROM clause are required for every SQL query. They must appear before any other clauses in a query. The result of a SQL query is always a table. The SELECT statement will probably be your most used SQL statement. It can take many forms, some simple, some complex. SELECT statements of many different types are shown as examples in the chapters that follow.

CREATE VIEW

In large databases containing large tables, it is much more likely that users will work with views than with complete tables. This might be a matter of security, where certain users are granted privileges only on views rather than on the whole table, and/or it might be a matter of convenience where there is no need to burden a user with having to make complicated queries of a whole table when the user only works with a small segment of it.

To create a view, you select only those columns from the base table (or tables) that you are interested in.

To define a view, you must give the view a name and then state the query containing the column names and specifications that will comprise the view. The syntax is:

```
CREATE VIEW <viewname>[<view_column_names>]
    AS <query expression>;
```

where <query expression> is a SELECT...FROM command.

Views are not stored. Instead, they are recomputed for each query referring to them. Techniques for reducing the overhead of this recomputation will be considered in chapter 11.

While most of the SQL operations that can be performed on tables can also be performed on views, some special rules apply to views due to the fact that their existence is dependent on the base table(s) from which they are drawn. A view can contain selected columns from one or more tables. There are special restrictions when you use an UPDATE, INSERT or DELETE command from a view drawn from more than one table. This, and other special characteristics of views will be discussed further in chapter 11.

The Data Control Language (DCL)

The Data Control Language (DCL) consists of a group of SQL statements for granting authorization for data access, for allocating space, for space definitions, and for auditing database use. Some of these commands represent functions of the database administrator (DBA). The ORACLE SQL DCL commands are: COMMIT, ROLLBACK, GRANT, REVOKE, LOCK TABLE, and AUDIT. Their syntaxes are shown in the next few sections.

COMMIT

The DCL command COMMIT is part of ORACLE's Transaction Processing Subsystem (TPS). A *transaction* is a logical unit of work, where each change affects or is affected by another change within the transaction. Changes to the database resulting from INSERT, DELETE or UPDATE commands should be made in groups that form logical transactions to ensure consistency and integrity of the data. At the end of such a transaction, a COMMIT statement should be entered so that the entire transaction will go into the database as a unit. Before the COMMIT statement is executed, the changes are visible only to the user making them; after the COMMIT statement is used, such changes are visible to all users. The syntax for the COMMIT statement is simply:

```
COMMIT [WORK];
```

Before a COMMIT statement is issued, the changes may be corrected, revised or eliminated (see ROLLBACK) without actually going into the database. After the COMMIT statement, such changes can only be corrected, revised or eliminated by issuing an INSERT, DELETE or UPDATE command. After a system failure, only committed changes will be saved.

You also can use ORACLE's AUTOCOMMIT option. This will cause every change to be committed as soon as it is entered. However, AUTOCOMMIT should only be used when the changes being made are logically unrelated. If it is used with logically related changes, the database might refuse to accept some changes because of the temporary inconsistencies they would cause.

Some SQL commands cause an automatic COMMIT. These are:

```
ALTER    CREATE
AUDIT    DISCONNECT
DROP     NOAUDIT
EXIT     QUIT
GRANT    REVOKE
```

ROLLBACK

The ROLLBACK command will cancel out changes that have been completed but not committed to the database. The syntax for ROLLBACK is:

```
ROLLBACK [WORK];
```

ROLLBACK is automatically performed when ORACLE recovers from a system failure. Also, certain errors, such as attempting to insert a bad record, a duplicate record, or an invalid number into a column, will cause ROLLBACK to execute. Syntax errors discovered during parsing will not cause a ROLLBACK.

GRANT

There are three forms of the GRANT command. The first form gives users access privileges to database objects. Initially, only a DBA can use this form of the GRANT command, except that any user can use it to change his or her own password. The syntax for the first form of GRANT is:

```
GRANT <database_priv> [,<database_priv>] ...
    TO <user> [,<user>] ...
    [IDENTIFIED BY <password> [,<password>] ... ];
```

where:

<database_priv> specifies one or more of the following database privileges (listed in increasing order of privilege):

CONNECT
RESOURCE
DBA

<user>	names either a new or existing database user name. If the name already exists in the database, then use this statement to add database privileges. If the name does not already exist, it is added to the data dictionary with the specified database privileges.
<password>	specifies a password for each user name. May be used to provide new passwords to new users or to change the password of an existing user. The password does not need to be specified if the GRANT statement is being used to add privileges to an existing user.

The second form of the GRANT command provides access to tablespaces with the option to impose a limit on the amount of space an individual user can use. This applies only to the RESOURCE privilege because the CONNECT privilege does not carry the right to access tablespaces, and the DBA privilege has all rights. The syntax for the second form of GRANT is:

```
GRANT RESOURCE [ (<quota> [K|M]) ]
ON <tablespace>
TO [PUBLIC | <user> [,<user>] ...];
```

where:

GRANT RESOURCE	specifies that the list of users can create objects in the specified tablespace.
<quota>	is shown as an integer and represents the number of bytes of space within the tablespace the user may allocate. No <quota> means an unlimited tablespace resource. The use of zero revokes quota or RESOURCE privilege on the tablespace. If <quota> is followed by K, then the quota is computed as the <quota> multiplied by 1024. If M is used, then the quota will be the <quota> multiplied by 1048576.
<user>	is an existing user name. The keyword PUBLIC can be used to grant the RESOURCE privilege to all database users.

The third form of the GRANT command is used to grant specific types of access to tables, views, and sequences. You must own the database object, have been granted GRANT OPTION on the object, or have the DBA privilege to use this form of the GRANT command. The syntax for third form of the GRANT command is:

```
GRANT <object_priv> [, <object_priv> ] ... | {ALL [PRIVILEGES]}
ON [<user.>] <object>
TO (<user> | PUBLIC) [,user] ...
[ WITH GRANT OPTION ];
```

where:

<object_priv>	for *tables*, <object_priv> is one of: ALTER, DELETE, INDEX, INSERT, REFERENCES, SELECT or UPDATE. For *views*, <object_priv> is one of: DELETE, INSERT, SELECT or UPDATE. For *sequences*, <object_priv> is either ALTER or SELECT. The UPDATE privilege can restrict updates to specific columns. The syntax for this privilege is:

```
UPDATE ( <column> [,<column>] ... )
```

where:

<column>	specifies a column from the <table>.
ALL PRIVILEGES	represents all privileges specified by <object_priv>.
ON [<user.>] <object>	specifies the table, view, or synonym on which the privilege(s) are granted.
TO <user(s)>	is one or more users being granted the privilege.
PUBLIC	represents all users, present and future.
WITH GRANT OPTION	specifies that the grantee may pass on the privileges that he has been granted to other users.

The table owner always has all privileges on the table. Access privileges are illustrated in chapter 9.

REVOKE

At any time, the DBA can withdraw any access privileges given with the GRANT statement. To do this, the DBA must use the REVOKE command. The syntax is:

```
REVOKE <privilege(s)> FROM <username>;
```

If the lowest level of privilege (CONNECT) is revoked, then all privileges are revoked. However, higher levels (RESOURCE or DBA) may be revoked while leaving the user the right to access with a lower level privilege.

Table 4-2 ORACLE SQL Keywords that May Become Reserved Words.

ARCHIVELOG, AUTHORIZATION

BACKUP, BEGIN

CACHE, CHARACTER, CLOSE, COBOL, COMMIT, CONSTRAINT, CONTENTS,

CONTINUE, CONTROLFILE, CRASH, CURSOR, CYCLE

DATABASE, DATAFILE, DEC, DECLARE, DISMOUNT, DOUBLE

END, ESCAPE, EVENTS, EXEC

FETCH, FOREIGN, FORTRAN, FOUND

GO, GOTO

INCLUDING, INDICATOR, INITRANS, INT

KEY

LANGUAGE, LINK, LOGFILE

MAXDATAFILES, MAXINSTANCES, MAXLOGFILES, MAXTRANS, MAXVALUE,

MINEXTENTS, MINVALUE, MODULE, MOUNT

NEXT, NOARCHIVELOG, NOCACHE, NOCYCLE, NOMAXVALUE, NOMINVALUE, NOORDER

NORMAL, NOSORT, NUMERIC

ONLY, OPEN

PASCAL, PCTINCREASE, PCTUSED, PL1, PRECISION, PRIMARY, PROCEDURE

READ, REAL, REFERENCES, RELEASE, RESETLOGS, REUSE, ROLLBACK

SAVEPOINT, SCHEMA, SECTION, SEGMENT, SEQUENCE, SHARED, SOME, SORT,

SPECIFIED, SQL, SQLCODE, SQLERROR, STATEMENT, STORAGE, SWITCH, SYSTEM

TABLES, TABLESPACE, TEMPORARY, TRANSACTION

USING, WRITE, WORK

LOCK TABLE

ORACLE has an elaborate locking system to avoid deadlocks. The default locking is shown in Table 4-3. If you don't specify any locks, the ORACLE Transaction Processing Subsystem (TPS) default locking system will lock tables and rows for certain SQL statements. At times, however, you might want to override this default locking, but you must own the table, have DBA privilege, or have been granted ALTER, DELETE, INSERT, SELECT or UPDATE on the table in order to override the TPS locking system. You can override the automatic locking with the LOCK TABLE command shown here:

```
LOCK TABLE [<user>.]<table> [, [<user>.]<table>] ...
IN <lockmode> MODE
[NOWAIT];
```

where:

<user>	is the owner of the table.
<table>	is an existing table to which you have access.
<lockmode>	is one of the following commands: ROW SHARE, ROW EXCLUSIVE, SHARE UPDATE, SHARE, SHARE ROW EXCLUSIVE or EXCLUSIVE.
NOWAIT	specifies that ORACLE should not wait for the table if the table has been locked by another user. Instead, ORACLE will return control to the user.

While the execution of SQL statements is affected by this locking system, it is not a part of SQL in ORACLE, therefore no further discussion of the locking system will be undertaken here. For further details see your *SQL*Plus User's Guide*.

Table 4-3 ORACLE Transaction Processing Subsystem Default Locking.

SQL Statement	Row Lock	Table Lock
SELECT	—no lock obtained—	
SELECT FOR UPDATE	X	RS
LOCK <table> IN <mode> MODE		
EXCLUSIVE (X)		X
SHARE UPDATE (RS)		RS
SHARE ROW EXCLUSIVE (SRX)		SRX
ROW SHARE		RS
ROW EXCLUSIVE		RX
SHARE		S
INSERT	X	
UPDATE	X	
DELETE	X	
DDL/DCL		X

AUDIT

The only users who can audit a given table, view or synonym are the object's owner and the DBA. The syntax of the AUDIT command is:

```
AUDIT {<t_option> [, <t_option>] ... | ALL }
ON { <tablename>| DEFAULT }
[ BY {ACCESS|SESSION }]
[WHENEVER [ NOT ] SUCCESSFUL ];
```

where:

<t_option>	is one of the following commands: ALTER, AUDIT, COMMENT, DELETE, GRANT, INDEX, INSERT, LOCK, RENAME, SELECT, UPDATE.
<tablename>	is the name of a view, base table or synonym denoting a view or base table.
DEFAULT	specifies that all tables created after this command will be audited by default in the modes specified by the <t_option> list.
BY ACCESS	specifies that one audit record per access per type of audit access be generated.
BY SESSION	specifies that only one audit record be generated per type of audit access for the duration of the user's session.
WHENEVER SUCCESSFUL	establishes an audit state in which SQL statements are audited only if they complete successfully.
WHENEVER NOT SUCCESSFUL	establishes an audit state in which SQL statements are audited only when they fail.

All auditing options are applicable to base tables. For views, you cannot use the ALTER or INDEX options.

Table expressions (clauses)

Table expressions are clauses that are used to derive tables. The common table expressions supported by SQL are:

FROM	names the table(s) from which rows are to be selected.
WHERE	specifies the condition(s) the selected rows must meet.
GROUP BY	separates the rows selected into specified groups.
HAVING	states the condition to be satisfied by each displayed group.
ORDER BY	specifies the order in which the selected rows will be displayed (either individually or within groups).

The FROM clause is required for a SQL query but the WHERE, GROUP BY, HAVING, and ORDER BY clauses are all optional. Table expressions are discussed in detail in chapter 5.

ORACLE SQL functions

SQL in ORACLE contains sets of functions that are used to manipulate individual data items. These functions accept zero or more arguments and return one or more results. (An *argument* is a user-supplied variable or constant.) The functions included in ORACLE SQL are character string, numeric string, date, aggregate (or group), and miscellaneous. They follow the format of:

```
<function_name> <argument1> [<,argument2> ,... <argumentN>]
```

ORACLE SQL functions are listed in the following sections and are illustrated in chapter 6.

Character string functions

The character string functions in ORACLE SQL and their syntaxes are:

```
CHARTOROWID<char>)
<column> || <column>
DECODE (<from>, <val>, <code>, <val>, <code>, ... <default>)
HEXTORAW(<char>)
INITCAP(<char>)
LENGTH (<char>)
LOWER (<char>)
RAWTOHEX(<raw>)
ROWIDTOCHAR(<rowid>)
SOUNDEX(<char>)
<string1> || <string2>
TO_CHAR(<n> [<fmt])
TO_NUMBER(<char>)
TRANSLATE(<oldstr,newstr>)
UPPER(<column>)
USERENV(<char>)
```

Numeric string functions

The numeric string functions and their syntaxes in ORACLE SQL are:

```
ABS(<n>)
CEIL(<n>)
FLOOR(<n>)
MOD(<m,n>)
POWER(<m,n>)
ROUND(<n[,m]>)
SIGN(<n>)
SQRT(<n>)
TRUNC(<n[,m]>)
```

Date functions

The date functions and their syntaxes in ORACLE SQL are:

```
<date + number>
<date + hours/(24)>
<date + minutes/(24*60)>
<date + seconds/(24*60*60)>
<date – number>
<date – hours/24>
<date – minutes/(24*60)>
<date – seconds/(24*60*60)>
<date – date>
<(date – date)*24>
```

Aggregate (group) functions

The aggregate functions of SQL are not contained in relational algebra, therefore SQL is considered to be more powerful than relational algebra in this respect. (See the book *Database System Concepts* by Henry Korth and Abraham Silberschatz for additional information on this subject. The Bibliography contains a reference for this book.)

ORACLE SQL contains the aggregate, or group functions Average (AVG), COUNT DISTINCT, COUNT(*), Maximum (MAX), Minimum (MIN), SUM, Standard Deviation (STDDEV), and VARIANCE. Each of the aggregate functions returns a single value for the group of values on which it operates.

The aggregate function goes in the SELECT statement of a query followed by the column name to which it applies. To avoid confusion, the column name is enclosed in parentheses. You can use more than one aggregate function in the same SELECT statement.

The syntax for using aggregate functions in a query is:

```
SELECT    <aggregate_function1>(<column_name>),
          [...,
          <aggregate functionN>(<column_name>)]
FROM      <table(s)>
WHERE     <condition(s)>;
```

Aggregate functions are illustrated in chapter 6.

Miscellaneous functions

Miscellaneous functions supported by ORACE SQL are:

```
DECODE(<expr,> <search1,> <result1,>[<search2,> <results2,>]
    ... [default]
DUMP
GREATEST(<expr> <,expr> ...)
LEAST(<expr> <,expr> ... )
NVL(<expr1,expr2>)
UID
USERENV(<option>)
VSIZE(<expr>)
```

NVL is the Null Value Function. UID is the unique integer assigned to each user name. VSIZE returns the number of bytes used to store ORACLE's internal representation of <expr>.

Subqueries

SQL provides for the use of subqueries (also called nested selects or subselects). These can be used to obtain information needed to complete the main query. This amounts to writing one compound query instead of two or more simple queries, and therefore provides a method for increasing efficiency.

In the processing of a compound SQL statement, ORACLE evaluates the subquery first, then applies the results to the main query. The most powerful uses of SQL are achieved by users who are skilled in setting up subqueries. ORACLE SQL imposes no limit on the number of subqueries that can be nested within one query.

If you know that the subquery should return at most only one value, or if you want to be certain that the result is unique, the syntax is:

```
SELECT    <columns>
FROM      <tables>
WHERE     <condition> <comparison predicate>
          (<subquery>);
```

The above syntax will return an error message if more than one row fits the condition.

On the other hand, if the subquery will (or could) return more than one value, then the syntax requires the IN predicate as follows:

```
SELECT    <columns>
FROM      <tables>
WHERE     <column_name> IN
                   (<subquery>);
```

More details on constructing subqueries, as well as some examples of them, appear in chapter 6.

Summary

This chapter gives an overview of the entire SQL syntax, including the catalog, the SQL commands, keywords, datatypes, value expressions, predicates, the Data Definition Language, Data Manipulation Language, Data Control Language, table expressions, logical connectives, SQL functions, and subqueries. It refers the reader to the chapters where each of these language elements is illustrated.

5
CHAPTER

Table expressions and predicates

The table expressions used to derive tables are the following: FROM, WHERE, GROUP BY, HAVING, and ORDER BY, which are discussed in this chapter.

The predicates used in SQL to place a specific condition on a query are:

- comparison (=, < >, <, >, < =, > =), BETWEEN, IN, LIKE, IS NULL, IS NOT NULL.
- quantified (ALL, SOME, ANY, and EXISTS.

These predicates are explained and illustrated later in this chapter.

Table expressions (clauses)

Table expressions are used to specify a table or a grouped table. These are clauses that are used to derive tables that are the result of the last specified clause. The table expressions are:

FROM

```
WHERE
GROUP BY
HAVING
ORDER BY
```

The FROM clause is necessary to a SQL query; the WHERE, GROUP BY, HAVING, and ORDER BY clauses are all optional.

FROM

The FROM clause specifies a table or tables from which the desired rows are to be retrieved. For example:

```
SELECT  *
FROM    Suppliers;
```

specifies that rows are to be retrieved with values in all columns from a Suppliers table.

A SQL query always returns a table. Therefore, the result of the FROM clause is always a table. If there are no optional table expressions in the query, such as WHERE, GROUP BY, HAVING or ORDER BY, then the retrieved table is the table composed of the columns in the target list only. It is called the *result table*.

If the table retrieved by the FROM clause is a grouped view, then the query cannot contain any optional table expressions such as WHERE, GROUP BY or HAVING. (See chapter 11 for further discussion of this point.)

If the target list contains columns from more than one table, then the FROM clause must name all of those tables in any order regardless of the order of the columns in the target list.

WHERE

The WHERE clause specifies a table derived by the application of a search condition to the tables listed in the FROM clause. In other words, the result of a WHERE clause is that row, or rows, retrieved from the tables named in the FROM clause that meets the WHERE clause specification. The syntax is:

```
SELECT  <column1>, <column2>, ..., <columnN>
FROM    <tablename>
WHERE   <condition>;
```

For example, if you want to send out a notice to all salespeople of your firm, but not to other members of the firm, you can select out the list of salespeople with the following command:

```
SELECT  employee_name, employee_no
FROM    Employees
WHERE   title = 'salesperson';
```

The WHERE clause may contain one or more subqueries. If it does, each subquery following the WHERE clause is executed for each row retrieved. (Subqueries are discussed in chapter 6.)

GROUP BY

The GROUP BY clause specifies a grouped table resulting from the application of the GROUP BY clause to the result of any previously specified clause.

The GROUP BY clause specifically references a column of the table named in the FROM clause and then groups rows on the basis of the values in that column.

The result of the GROUP BY clause partitions the result of the FROM clause into a set of groups so that for each group of more than one row, the values in the grouping column are identical. The syntax is:

```
SELECT       <column1>, <column2>, ..., <column N>
FROM         <tablename>
GROUP BY     <grouping_column>;
```

For example, suppose Table 5-1 is a list of all your suppliers, but you would like to have these separated according to city. Then you would enter:

```
SELECT       *
FROM         Suppliers
GROUP BY     city;
```

The result of this query would be a listing of the suppliers grouped so that each set retrieved would be a set of suppliers located in the same city, as shown here:

Suppliers Name	Part No.	Part Name	City	Unit Price
Acme	38	Valve	New York	5.00
Ziptools	2	Hose	New York	3.00
Best	15	Filter	Chicago	4.00
Handy	6	Valve	Chicago	3.00
Central	18	Piston	Chicago	8.00
Joe's	74	Piston	Wichita	6.00
First	9	Hose	Mobile	2.00
Quiktool	22	Filter	Mobile	4.00
ABC	8	Valve	Mobile	3.00

The GROUP BY clause cannot be used when the table resulting from the FROM clause is a grouped view. (See chapter 11 for details on views.)

If the command does not contain a WHERE clause, then the GROUP BY clause is placed immediately after the FROM clause. If the command has a

WHERE clause, then the GROUP BY clause goes after the WHERE clause.

The rows returned will be ordered randomly within each group because the GROUP BY clause does not do any ordering.

HAVING

The HAVING clause specifies a restriction on the grouped table resulting from the previous GROUP BY clause, and eliminates groups not meeting the condition it specifies. If HAVING is specified in a query, then GROUP BY also must be specified.

HAVING is used to specify the quality a group must possess for it to be returned. HAVING compares a property of the group with a constant value. It performs the same function for groups that WHERE performs for individual rows. In other words, HAVING eliminates non-qualifying groups, in the same way that WHERE eliminates non-qualifying rows. HAVING is therefore always used with GROUP BY. The syntax is:

```
SELECT      <column1>, <column2>, ..., <columnN>
FROM        <tablename>
GROUP BY    <grouping_column>
HAVING      <specified_group_property>;
```

Referring to Table 5-1, if you want to select only those suppliers where there are more than two suppliers in the same city, set up the query:

```
SELECT      <name>, <city>
FROM        <suppliers>
GROUP BY    <city>
HAVING      COUNT(*) > 2;
```

Table 5-1 Suppliers.

Name	Part No.	Part Name	City	Unit Price
ABC	8	Valve	Mobile	3.00
Acme	38	Valve	New York	5.00
Best	15	Filter	Chicago	4.00
Central	18	Piston	Chicago	8.00
First	9	Hose	Mobile	2.00
Handy	6	Valve	Chicago	3.00
Joe's	74	Piston	Wichita	6.00
Quiktool	22	Filter	Mobile	4.00
Ziptools	2	Hose	New York	3.00

The following result table will be returned:

Name	City
Best	Chicago
Handy	Chicago

Name	City
Central	Chicago
First	Mobile
Quiktool	Mobile
ABC	Mobile

The HAVING clause is always placed after the GROUP BY clause. Examples of other uses of HAVING are shown in the section on aggregate functions and the section on subqueries, both in chapter 6.

ORDER BY

The ORDER BY clause allows you to specify the order in which rows will appear in the retrieval. Whereas, GROUP BY merely places together all rows that have the same value in a specified column, ORDER BY lists the rows within a specified group according to increasing or decreasing value.

If the ORDER BY clause is used, it must be the last clause in a SELECT command.

Ascending (ASC) or descending (DESC) order may be specified, but because ASC is the default ordering, it is usually only necessary to specify the direction if DESC is desired.

If the ordering column consists of letters rather than numbers, SQL will use ascending alphabetic order (starting with A) if DESC is not specified.

For example, the following command can be used to order suppliers alphabetically:

```
SELECT       supplier_name, part_no, part_name
FROM         Suppliers
ORDER BY     supplier_name;
```

This command would result in an alphabetic ordering of the suppliers starting with those names beginning with "A," as shown here:

Suppliers Name	Part_No	Part Name
ABC	8	Valve
Acme	38	Valve
Best	15	Filter
Central	18	Piston
First	9	Hose
Handy	6	Valve
Joe's	74	Piston
Quiktool	22	Filter
Ziptools	2	Hose

You also can use ORDER BY for more than one column. For example, the above query could be written as follows:

```
SELECT      supplier_name, part_no, part_name
FROM        Suppliers
ORDER BY    supplier_name, part_no;
```

In this case the first ordering will be alphabetical in ascending order, and part numbers will be shown in ascending order within each alphabetical listing. For the list shown above, the two-column ordering would not change the result table, but note that ordering two columns does affect the next example.

To achieve a descending order, put the DESC after the column name. For example, to list suppliers starting with those who sell the most expensive parts and ending with those who sell the least expensive ones, you would use the following query:

```
SELECT      supplier_name, part_name, price
FROM        suppliers
ORDER BY    price DESC, supplier_name;
```

This will list all suppliers by price starting with the highest price and working on down to the lowest, and within each price, the suppliers will be ordered alphabetically in ascending order, as shown here:

Suppliers

Supplier Name	Part Name	Price
Central	Piston	8.00
Joe's	Piston	6.00
Acme	Valve	5.00
Best	Filter	4.00
Quiktool	Filter	4.00
ABC	Valve	3.00
Handy	Valve	3.00
Ziptools	Hose	3.00
First	Hose	2.00

Predicates

Predicates are conditions that are stated in the WHERE clause of a SQL query. The predicates supported by ORACLE SQL are shown in Table 5-2. They are comparison, BETWEEN, IN, LIKE, IS NULL, IS NOT NULL, quantified, and EXISTS, each of which is discussed and illustrated in the sections that follow.

Table 5-2 Predicates.

Operator	**Meaning**
Comparison:	
=	equal to
!=	not equal to
>	greater than
>=	greater than or equal to
<	less than
<=	less than or equal to
BETWEEN ... AND ...	between two values
IN (list)	any of a list of values
LIKE	match a character pattern
IS NULL	is a null value

To negate the last four operators, use the operator NOT: NOT BETWEEN, NOT IN, NOT LIKE, and IS NOT NULL.

Comparison predicate

A comparison predicate specifies a comparison of two values. It consists of a value expression followed by a comparison operator followed by either another value expression or a single-valued subquery. The datatypes of the two value expressions, or the value expression and the subquery, must be comparable.

The comparison operators supported by SQL are:

equals =
not equal to < >
less than <
greater than >
less than or equal to < =
greater than or equal to > =

If the values on both sides of a comparison operator are not NULL, then the comparison predicate is either true or false. For example:

```
321003 < > 123003
'March 21, 1988' = 'March 21, 1988'
520 > 519
0 < 2
```

If either of the two value expressions is a NULL value, or if the subquery is empty, then the result of the comparison predicate is unknown. However, when GROUP BY, ORDER BY or DISTINCT are used in conjunction with a comparison predicate, one NULL value is identical to, or is a duplicate of, another NULL value.

Character strings may be compared by means of the previously mentioned comparison operators. This is accomplished by comparing characters in the same ordinal positions in the string. Thus, two character strings are equal if all characters with the same ordinal position are equal. For example:

```
'London' = 'London'
'London' <> 'New York'
'52-I-432' <> '521432FM'
```

BETWEEN predicate

The BETWEEN predicate specifies a range comparison. The syntax is:

```
...BETWEEN...AND...
```

or

```
...NOT BETWEEN...AND...
```

where each ellipsis contains a value. The datatypes of the values must be comparable. For example, to select parts priced between $5 and $10 from Table 5-1, enter:

```
SELECT   part_no, part_name, price, supplier
FROM     Suppliers
WHERE    price BETWEEN 5 AND 10;
```

This will return the following result table:

PART_NO	PART_NAME	PRICE	SUPPLIER
74	piston	6	Joe's
38	valve	5	Acme
18	piston	8	Central

(Note that because no ordering was specified, the rows returned will be in random order.)

The term NOT also may be used with BETWEEN to retrieve information outside of a range rather than inside the range. For example, to retrieve information only on parts priced below $3 and above $6, enter:

```
SELECT   part_no, part_name, price, supplier
FROM     Suppliers
WHERE    price NOT BETWEEN 3 AND 6;
```

The result of this query is:

PART_NO	PART NAME	PRICE	SUPPLIER
9	hose	2	First
18	piston	8	Central

IN (or NOT IN) predicate

The IN (or NOT IN) predicate specifies a *quantified comparison*. It lists a set of values and then tests for whether a candidate value is in that list. The list must be enclosed in parentheses. For example, to retrieve information on parts priced at $4, $5, and $7, enter:

```
SELECT   part_no, part_name, price, supplier
FROM     Suppliers
WHERE    price IN (4,5,7);
```

The result is:

PART_NO	PART NAME	PRICE	SUPPLIER
15	filter	4	Best
22	filter	4	Quiktool
38	valve	5	Acme

You could have written this query using OR instead of IN, as follows:

```
SELECT   part_no, part_name, price, supplier
FROM     Suppliers
WHERE    price = 4
OR       price = 5
OR       price = 7;
```

The result of this query is the same as the result shown for the query using IN.

The query also can be written using ANY:

```
SELECT   part_no, part_name, price, supplier
FROM     Suppliers
WHERE    price = ANY (4, 5, 7);
```

Again, the result is the same as the result shown for the query using IN.

The order in which the items in the list are shown in the query determines the order in which the columns will be displayed in the retrieval. It does not determine the order in which the rows will be displayed. If you want the retrieved rows to appear in a specific order, then the WHERE clause must be followed by an ORDER BY clause indicating the column variable on which the ordering should be based. The spaces between the items in the list are optional and will not affect the result.

The IN predicate can be negated by the use of NOT IN. For example, to obtain part numbers other than those contained in the set 4, 5, and 7, enter:

```
SELECT   part_no, part_name, price, supplier
FROM     suppliers
WHERE    price NOT IN (4, 5, 7);
```

The result will show every existing part number except parts numbered 4, 5, and 7.

LIKE (or NOT LIKE) predicate

The LIKE predicate specifies a pattern-matching comparison where an underscore (_) is used to represent a single character in the pattern, and a percent sign (%) is used to represent a character-string of arbitrary length (including zero). These symbols are called *wild cards* or "don't care" symbols. You can use them in cases where your information is incomplete.

The form of the LIKE predicate is:

```
<column_name> LIKE <character_string_constant>
```

LIKE can only be used with character string or graphic data, not with numeric data. For example, if you need the name and address of a supplier and are uncertain whether the company name is Reid or Read, you can enter:

```
SELECT   name, city
FROM     Suppliers
WHERE    name LIKE 'Re_d';
```

Use of the underscore indicates that you are uncertain of only one character.

If you are unsure whether the name is Redenbacker or Redinburger, then you would use the percent sign (%) as follows:

```
SELECT   name, city
FROM     Suppliers
WHERE    name LIKE 'Red%';
```

To reduce the vast number of retrievals that might occur, enter:

```
SELECT   name, city
FROM     Suppliers
WHERE    name LIKE 'Red_nb%er';
```

This indicates certainty on the position of the n but uncertainty on the one letter between the d and the n, certainty on the b following the n and uncertainty on the number and identity of the characters before the final er.

These two symbols can be used in a wide variety of ways, either individually or in combination with each other. They also can be used with NOT, which will exclude retrievals in a certain form. For example, if you are looking for a name that you know does not include the character string del, the predicate can be expressed as:

```
WHERE name NOT LIKE '%del%'
```

This excludes a name with that exact combination of letters, in that order, regardless of where del occurred in the name. It does not however, exclude the possibility that any of the individual letters d, e or l, might occur within the name. To exclude the occurrence of any of the individual letters in the retrieved name, you would have to exclude them individually because the clause shown here will only exclude that exact character string.

NULL predicate

The NULL predicate specifies a test for a NULL value. To query the database about a NULL value requires a slightly different approach than querying about any other value because of the special properties embodied in the NULL concept.

For example, if you are looking for a part name where, because of incomplete information, the price has been entered as NULL, you cannot specify:

```
WHERE price = NULL
```

because nothing, not even NULL itself, is equal to the NULL value. (This rule does not always hold throughout the SQL syntax. See, for example, the treatment of NULL values with SELECT DISTINCT, UNIQUE, and ORDER BY.) Also, you cannot use NULL in a SELECT clause.

You cannot find the NULL value by exclusion, as for example, by stipulating that the price is above or below any known price in the list. For example, if $10 is the highest specified price in the list, the query:

```
SELECT    part_name, price
FROM      Suppliers
WHERE     price > 10;
```

would not retrieve the part name with the NULL value, nor would the predicate:

```
WHERE price < 0
```

The only predicate allowed when searching for a NULL value is:

```
WHERE <column_specification> IS NULL
```

To exclude a NULL value, the syntax is:

```
WHERE <column_specification> IS NOT NULL
```

Therefore, to retrieve the names of suppliers where the price of the part supplied has been entered in the database as NULL, enter:

```
SELECT    supplier_name
FROM      Suppliers
WHERE     price IS NULL;
```

To retrieve the names of the suppliers where the price of the part has been entered in the database as a value other than NULL, enter:

```
SELECT    supplier_name
FROM      Suppliers
WHERE     price IS NOT NULL;
```

No other syntax will retrieve the desired target list when the NULL predicate is involved.

Quantified predicates ALL, SOME, and ANY

The quantified predicates ALL, SOME, and ANY require the use of a comparison predicate applied to the results of a subquery. A *comparison predicate* is a predicate containing a comparison operator such as equals (=), less than (<), greater than (>), less than or equal to (< =), greater than or equal to (> =), and not equal (< >), as explained in the "Comparison predicate" section of this chapter.

These predicates allow you to test a single value against all of the members of a set. For example, you might want to find the suppliers whose prices are lower than all the suppliers in Chicago. To do so, enter:

```
SELECT    supplier_name
FROM      Suppliers
WHERE     price < ALL
          (SELECT price
          FROM    Suppliers
          WHERE   city = 'Chicago');
```

Similarly, all the other comparison operators may be combined with SOME, ANY, and ALL. However, when the comparison operator being used is equals (=), the term ANY is interchangeable with IN, and sometimes it might seem more logical to use IN.

In many cases ANY has the same meaning as SOME. Consider the query "Find all suppliers with a price lower than some supplier in Chicago." You can write this as:

```
SELECT    supplier_name
FROM      Suppliers
WHERE     price < ANY
          (SELECT price
          FROM  Suppliers
          WHERE city = 'Chicago');
```

The < ANY comparison in the WHERE clause of the outer SELECT is true if the price is less than at least one member of the set of all suppliers in Chicago.

EXISTS predicate

The EXISTS predicate states the condition(s) for an empty set. It contains a subquery (see chapter 6 for a discussion of subqueries) that, together with the stipulation EXISTS, can be evaluated to either true or false. If the result of the subquery exists, for example if it contains at least one row, then the predicate is true. If the result of the subquery does not exist, then the set described by the subquery is empty.

From the previous paragraph it is apparent that the predicate EXISTS represents the existential quantifier of formal logic. The universal quantifier of formal logic, FORALL, is not directly supported by the ORACLE SQL language, however, it will be shown that an equivalent predicate using EXISTS will produce the same result as what could be obtained with FORALL.

The predicate EXISTS can be used wherever a query using the predicate IN can be used. (But the inverse is not true, IN cannot always be used where EXISTS can be used.) Because queries using EXISTS are sometimes easier to formulate than queries using IN, the use of EXISTS takes on added importance in SQL.

The general syntax for the EXISTS predicate is:

```
SELECT    <column_name>
FROM      <tablename>
WHERE     EXISTS (<subquery>);
```

Only the general form of the EXISTS subquery is shown here. Subqueries are discussed in detail in chapter 6.

A query also may be phrased using NOT EXISTS with the same syntax by adding the NOT after the WHERE in the outer SELECT:

```
...
WHERE NOT EXISTS
          (SELECT*
          FROM      <tablename>
          WHERE     <condition(s)>);
```

The predicate form NOT EXISTS also may be used to obtain the result obtainable with the universal quantifier FORALL, which is not available in SQL, by using the double negative:

```
NOT (EXISTS <variable> (NOT (<variable contained in constant>)))
```

This is best explained by the use of an alias, which is discussed in chapter 6.

Summary

In this chapter, table expressions and predicates were illustrated. This includes the following clauses: FROM, WHERE, GROUP BY, HAVING, ORDER

BY, the comparison predicates BETWEEN, IN, NOT IN, LIKE, NOT LIKE, IS NULL, IS NOT NULL, and the quantified predicates ALL, SOME, ANY, and EXISTS.

Chapter 5 exercises

5.1 Write a SQL query to retrieve all columns and rows of the Supplier tables.

Write the FROM clause, and wherever necessary the WHERE clause and/or other table expressions, for each of the following:

5.2 For suppliers with a price lower than $5.

5.3 For a list of all suppliers, with the part numbers in ascending order.

5.4 For suppliers of valves, in alphabetical order.

5.5 For a supplier whose name starts with H and ends with y.

5.6 For a supplier whose name is either Quiktool or Quicktool.

5.7 For suppliers in either New York, Atlanta or Denver.

5.8 For part numbers 8, 9 or 10.

5.9 For suppliers where the part number has been entered as NULL.

5.10 For suppliers where the part number has been filled in with a value other than NULL.

Answers to chapter 5 exercises

5.1
```
SELECT *
FROM  Suppliers;
```

5.2
```
FROM Suppliers
WHERE  price < 5;
```

5.3
```
FROM Suppliers
ORDER BY part_no;
```

5.4
```
FROM Suppliers
WHERE  part_name = 'valves'
ORDER BY supplier_name;
```

5.5
```
FROM Suppliers
WHERE  supplier_name = 'H%y';
```

5.6
```
FROM Suppliers
WHERE  supplier_name = 'Qui%ktool';
```

5.7 FROM Suppliers
WHERE supplier_name IN ('New York', 'Atlanta',
'Denver');

5.8 FROM Suppliers
WHERE part_no BETWEEN '8' AND '10';

5.9 FROM Suppliers
WHERE part_no IS NULL;

5.10 FROM Suppliers
WHERE part_no IS NOT NULL;

6
CHAPTER

Logical connectives, SQL functions, and subqueries

SQL is designed to make use of the Boolean operators INTERSECTION, UNION, and MINUS. ORACLE makes full use of these operators. This chapter will also discuss the use of the SQL functions: character, numeric, date, aggregate, and miscellaneous.

Subqueries (also called subselects or nested queries) which have been referred to briefly earlier, will be illustrated in the latter part of this chapter.

Logical connectives

With SQL, you can achieve all the results of the three operations of relational algebra: intersect, union, and minus. Intersection is achieved by the use of AND. Union is accomplished by using OR. Minus is achieved by using the word MINUS, and can be handled indirectly by using EXISTS and NOT EXISTS. MINUS also can be obtained by using IN and NOT IN. These logical connectives are illustrated in the next five sections.

AND (INTERSECTION)

The AND in ORACLE SQL has the same meaning and usage as the intersection of relational algebra. It is used to set up a query where there are two conditions that must be met for the query to return one or more rows. You can use AND as follows:

```
SELECT   <columns>
FROM     <tablename>
WHERE    <condition1>
AND      <condition2>;
```

For example, using the list of suppliers shown in Table 5-1, in chapter 5, let's assume you want to find suppliers who sell parts with numbers higher than 12, and are located in Chicago. Set up the query as follows:

```
SELECT   supplier_name, part_no
FROM     Suppliers
WHERE    part_no > 12
AND      city = 'Chicago';
```

This will return only those rows that satisfy both the first and second condition, as shown here:

Supplier Name	Part_no
Best	15
Central	18

This example uses the AND operator with two columns; it also can be used with more than two columns, and it can be used in conjunction with OR to form more complex queries. These uses will be exhibited in the section entitled "Using AND and OR in the same query," after the use of OR has been illustrated.

OR (UNION)

The Boolean UNION is represented in SQL by the term OR. It is the case where either one or both of two conditions are met. (However, UNION and OR are not synonymous. OR cannot form the union of two tables because you must always use OR in a WHERE clause. On the other hand, you cannot put UNION in a WHERE clause.)

Except for the substitution of the word OR for the AND, the SELECT statement will look exactly like that shown for INTERSECTION, but the results might be very different depending on the contents of the database. The SQL query using OR for the union is:

```
SELECT   <columns>
FROM     <tablename>
WHERE    <condition1>
OR       <condition2>;
```

The rows returned will be those meeting either condition1 or condition2, or both. When rows are returned using OR, the result may or may not be the same as when AND is used. For example, using the same query as in the earlier section entitled "Logical connectives," but substituting OR for AND, you get the query:

```
SELECT   supplier_name, part_no, city
FROM     Suppliers
WHERE    city = 'Chicago'
OR       part_no > 12;
```

which will give the following result table:

Supplier name	Part_no	City
Acme	38	New York
Best	15	Chicago
Central	18	Chicago
Joe's	74	Wichita
Quiktool	22	Mobile

Using AND and OR in the same query

When using AND and OR in the same query, you should use parentheses to make the meaning clear. The placement of the parentheses can completely change the result. For example,

```
SELECT   supplier_name, part_no
FROM     Suppliers
WHERE    city = 'Dallas'
AND      part_name = 'valve'
AND      (part_no = 15 OR part_no = 74);
```

This will return all Dallas suppliers of valves numbered 15 or 74. Contrast this with the following query:

```
SELECT   supplier_name, part_no
FROM     Suppliers
```

```
WHERE    city = 'Dallas'
AND      (part_name = 'valve' AND part_no = 15)
OR       part_no = 74;
```

This returns all Dallas suppliers of valves with part number 15, and all Dallas suppliers of parts numbered 74 whether or not these parts were valves. Therefore, the placement of the parentheses is important in making the meaning clear. In addition, ORACLE SQL has assigned precedence values to operators, with NOT having the highest precedence, followed by AND, then OR. The safest approach is to use parentheses wherever possible to clarify your intent.

The MINUS (Difference) operator

The MINUS operator can be used to retrieve rows that meet one condition while excluding another. It is set up to eliminate a condition rather than to add one. For example, if you wanted to find the suppliers of Part No. 30 who are not located in Chicago, you could set it up this way:

```
SELECT   supplier_name, part_no, city
FROM     Suppliers
WHERE    part_no = 30
MINUS
SELECT   supplier_name, part_no, city
FROM     Suppliers
WHERE    city = 'Chicago';
```

The datatypes, and their widths, in the previous two SELECT statements must match. The result is only those rows retrieved by the first SELECT that do not match those retrieved by the second SELECT.

The same result can be obtained by using NOT. For example, to find the suppliers of Part No. 30 who are not located in Chicago, you could enter:

```
SELECT   supplier_name, part_no, city
FROM     Suppliers
WHERE    NOT city = 'Chicago'
AND      part_no = 30;
```

which would give the same result as the query above using MINUS. You could also write the WHERE clause:

```
WHERE     city <> 'Chicago';
```

But you cannot use:

```
WHERE     city NOT = 'Chicago';
```

Substituting IN and NOT IN for AND, OR or MINUS

The IN and NOT IN connectives are used to test for membership in a class, or to exclude members of a specified class. Obviously, it is sometimes possible to use these interchangeably with the AND, OR or MINUS operators.

One procedure is to list the class members, and specify whether the result is to be in or not in that list, as follows:

```
SELECT   supplier_name, part_no, city
FROM     Suppliers
WHERE    city IN ('New_York', 'Atlanta', 'Boston');
```

This command will retrieve the specified columns for all suppliers in the three cities named. This is the same result you would get if you worded the command as follows:

```
SELECT   supplier_name, part_no, city
FROM     Suppliers
WHERE    city = 'New_York'
OR       city = 'Atlanta'
OR       city = 'Boston';
```

Clearly, the command using IN is much simpler and shorter than the one using OR.

The connective NOT IN will exclude the values within the parentheses. For example, the query shown earlier in the section entitled "MINUS" stated "Find the suppliers of Part No. 30 who are not located in Chicago." This query could be entered as:

```
SELECT   supplier_name, part_no, city
FROM     Suppliers
WHERE    part_no = 30
AND      city NOT IN ('Chicago');
```

The result is the same as it would be if you entered:

```
SELECT   supplier_name, part_no, city
FROM     Suppliers
WHERE    part_no = 30
MINUS
SELECT   supplier_name, part_no, city
FROM     Suppliers
WHERE    city = 'Chicago';
```

It could also be entered as:

```
WHERE part_no = 30
AND   NOT (city = 'Chicago');
```

But, it cannot be entered as:

```
WHERE  part_no = 30
AND    city NOT = 'Chicago';
```

In general, when using NOT to exclude a condition, for example in place of the word "except," enclose the set to be excluded in parentheses, and precede the set with NOT. This form is necessary because SQL arose out of predicate calculus where the equal sign (=) and the quantities before and after it constitute a predicate, and while NOT can modify a predicate, it cannot be a part of a predicate.

Other uses of the NOT connective are shown with the BETWEEN predicate, and with LIKE in chapter 5.

Character string functions

Character string functions may be used in the SELECT command, the WHERE clause, and the ORDER BY clause. These functions will not change the internal data.

Table 6-1 contains the SQL character string functions. The DECODE function translates coded entries into the meanings of the code. For exam-

Table 6-1 Character String Functions.

Function	**Purpose**
CHARTOROWID (<char>)	Converts a CHAR value to a row ID.
<Column> ¦¦ <Column>	Concatenates columns with no intervening blanks.
DECODE (<from>, <val>, <code>, <val>, <code>, ... default)	If <from> equals any <val>, returns the following code; if not, returns default. <from> may be any datatype; <val> must be same type. Value returned is forced to the same datatype as the first <code>.
HEXTORAW (<char>)	Converts a CHAR value containing hexadecimal digits to a binary value (suitable for inclusion in a RAW column.)
INITCAP (<char>)	Capitalizes first letter of each word.
LENGTH (<char>)	Outputs the length of the string.
LOWER (<char>)	All letters forced to lowercase.
LPAD (<char1,n> [,<char2>])	Left padded to length <n> with the sequence of characters in <char2>; <char2> defaults to blanks.
LTRIM (<char> [,<set>])	Remove characters from the left: <char>, with initial characters removed up to the first character not in <set>. <Set> default to ''.

Table 6-1 Continued

Function	**Purpose**
RAWTOHEX (<raw>)	Converts a raw value to a CHAR value containing a hexadecimal number.
ROWIDTOCHAR (<rowid>)	Converts a row ID to a CHAR value.
RPAD (<char1,n> [,<char2>])	<char1>, right-padded to length <n> with the characters in <char2> replicated as many times as necessary; if <char2> is omitted, with blanks.
RTRIM(<char,>[<set>])	<char>, with final characters removed after the last character not in <set>. <Set> is optional; it defaults to ''.
SOUNDEX (<char>)	A CHAR value representing the sound of the word(s) in CHAR.
<String1> ¦¦ <String2>	Concatenates strings of characters with no intervening blanks.
TO_CHAR(<n>[,<fmt>])	Converts <n> to a CHAR value in the format specified. If <fmt> is omitted, <n> is converted to a CHAR value exactly long enough to hold the significant digits.
TO_NUMBER(<char>)	Converts a CHAR value containing a number to a number.
TRANSLATE(<oldstr>,<newstr>)	Substitutes the character in the <newstr> for the corresponding character in the <oldstr>.
UPPER(<column>)	Changes lowercase characters to uppercase.
USERENV(<char>)	Returns information about the user that is useful in writing an application-specific audit trail table. If <char> is ENTRYID, returns an available auditing entry identifier; if SESSIONID, returns user's auditing session identifier; if TERMINAL, returns user's terminal operating system identifier.

ple, suppose that you have a table called Stores, where the stores are coded as (1) large, (3) medium, and (5) small. If you wanted a meaningful listing of the stores according to size, you would want the decoded values shown. You would do this by entering the following command:

```
SELECT storeno, size
    DECODE(size, 'large' ,1, 'medium', 3,'small' ,5, 2)
    store_size
FROM    Stores;
```

If there are stores in your list that do not have the listed classifications, but have some other classification (such as "very small" or "medium to large") the number two in the DECODE statement ensures that all of these stores will be included under the default code number two.

You can use the DECODE function for any type of decoding: grade point numbers into arithmetic expressions, job codes into job titles, part numbers into part names, etc.

The arguments of the DECODE command determine:

1. The column to be decoded (storeno)
2. The original and translated values in the column ("large", 1,) etc.
3. Any default value into which original values that are not specified in your DECODE statement are to be decoded (2).

Numeric string functions

Numeric string functions may be used in the SELECT command, the WHERE clause, and the ORDER BY clause. Table 6-2 lists and explains the numeric string functions.

Table 6-2 Numeric String Functions.

Function	Description
ABS(<n>)	Absolute value of <n>.
CEIL(<n>)	Smallest integer greater than or equal to <n>.
FLOOR(<n>)	Largest integer equal to or less than <n>.
MOD(<m,n>)	Remainder of <m> divided by <n>.
POWER(<m,n>)	<m> raised to the <nth> power.
ROUND(<n>[,<m>])	<n> rounded to <m> decimal places; <m> may be positive or negative. If <m> is omitted, round to 0 places. If <m> is negative, round to the left of the decimal point. If <m> is positive, round to the right of the decimal point.
SIGN(<n>)	If <n> <0, −1; if <n> = 0, 0; if <n> > 0, 1.
SQRT(<n>)	Returns the positive square root of <n>. If <n> < 0, NULL.
TRUNC(<n>[,<m>])	<n> truncated to <m> decimal places; if <m> is omitted, to 0 places. If <m> is negative, leave 0 left of the decimal point.

The ROUND function rounds off a number to a specified number of decimal places. For example, if you wanted to calculate the average daily profit for each store during a 30-day month, with the results rounded to the nearest penny, you would set it up this way:

```
SELECT   sname, profit, profit/30, ROUND(profit/30,2)
FROM     Stores;
```

ROUND(profit/30,2) means that you want the result rounded to two decimal places. If the query asked for ROUND(profit/30,0) this would mean that you wanted the amount rounded to the nearest dollar (or the nearest whole integer).

The TRUNC function cuts off (truncates) numbers to a specified number of decimal places without rounding them. For example, if you truncate 56.99 to an integer, the result is 56, whereas if you ROUND 56.99 to an integer, the result is 57.

Set up the query using TRUNC just as you set up the query using ROUND:

```
SELECT    sname, profit, profit/30, TRUNC(profit/30,0)
FROM      Stores;
```

TRUNC(profit/30,0) means cut off all numbers after the decimal point. But keep in mind that the final results can be very different from results that are rounded.

Date functions

The default date format is DD-MON-YY for both input and output. The date datatype contains century, year, month, day, hour, minutes and seconds as shown in Table 6-3.

Table 6-3 Date Functions.

Function	**Purpose**
<date + number>	Adds a number of days
<date + hours/(24)>	Adds a number of hours
<date + minutes/(24*60)>	Adds a number of minutes
<date + seconds/(24*60*60)>	Adds a number of seconds
<date − number>	Subtracts a number of days
<date − hours/24>	Subtracts a number of hours
<date − minutes/(24*60)>	Subtracts a number of minutes
<date − seconds/(24*60*60)>	Subtracts a number of seconds
<date − date>	Determines number of days between
<(date − date)*24>	Determines number of hours between

You must always add/subtract a number of days and/or fractional days to a date field.

In order to display time, the TO_CHAR function must be used. Notice that MI stands for minutes and MM stands for months.

SYSDATE is a reserved word that can be used to represent today's date in any type of SQL statement, such as SELECT, INSERT, and UPDATE.

You can perform arithmetic on date fields, as follows:

date + number   Adds a number of days to a day and produces the resulting date.

date – number	Subtracts a number of days from a date and produces the resulting date.
date – date	Subtracts one date from another and produces the resulting number of days.

Aggregate (group) functions

Aggregate functions apply to groups of records. They summarize a column of values and return a single value. All aggregate functions can be applied to numeric values. Only the aggregate functions MIN, MAX, and COUNT can be applied to character and date values.

The aggregate functions supported by ORACLE are shown in Table 6-4.

Table 6-4 Aggregate Functions (can be used only in SELECT commands and subsequences).

Function	**Description**
AVG([DISTINCT¦ALL] <n>)	Average value of <n>, ignoring null values.
COUNT([DISTINCT¦ALL] <expr>)	Number of times <expr> evaluates to something other than NULL.
COUNT(*)	Returns the number of rows in the table, including those with nulls.
MAX([DISTINCT¦ALL] <expr>)	Maximum value of <expr>.
MIN([DISTINCT¦ALL] <expr>)	Minimum value of <expr>.
STDDEV([DISTINCT¦ALL] <expr>)	Standard deviation of <expr>, ignoring null values.
SUM([DISTINCT¦ALL] <n>)	Sum of values of <n>.
VARIANCE([DISTINCT¦ALL] <expr>)	Variance of <expr>, ignoring null values.

To find the average of a column of values, use the function AVG. For example, to find the average salary of cashiers, enter:

```
SELECT AVG(sal)
FROM     Employees
WHERE    title = 'cashier';
```

All the rows that satisfy the condition WHERE TITLE = 'cashier' will be used to calculate the average. This query will return a single value, AVG(sal).

You can use more than one group function in a SELECT command. For example:

```
SELECT AVG(sal), AVG(comm)
FROM     Employees
WHERE    title = 'salesman';
```

This returns the average salary and the average commission of all employees with the job title 'salesman'.

The COUNT function counts the number of non-null values, distinct values, or rows selected by the query.

If you want to count the number of unique items in a list, for example eliminating duplicates, then use the term DISTINCT. For example, if you want to count the number of different job titles held by a large group of employees, many of whom have the same title, you would set up the query this way:

```
SELECT   COUNT (DISTINCT title)
FROM     Employees
WHERE    city = 'chicago';
```

This command will eliminate duplicate values before the values are counted. When DISTINCT is used, only the unique values in the column will be in the computation.

There is a special form of count, COUNT(*) which will count the number of rows satisfying the conditions in the WHERE clause. For example, to count the number of employees in a specific department, the query would be:

```
SELECT   COUNT(*)
FROM     Employees
WHERE    dept = 'sales';
```

It is important to be aware of null values when you use aggregate functions because the effects of the null values will be hidden in the results. You will get different results depending on how ORACLE treats the null values. The null value function (NVL) is useful for guaranteeing that you get the type of result you want. It is treated in detail in a later section in this chapter.

Group functions versus individual functions

When you put a group function in a SELECT command, you cannot put an individual function in that same command. For example, if your command begins SELECT name, then you cannot follow this with AVG(sal). The column "name" has a value for each row selected, while AVG(SAL) has a single value for the whole query. If you combine a group function with an individual function, ORACLE will return an error message. However, there are two exceptions to the above rule:

1. You can request individual results based on a group function in a subquery, or group results based on individual selections in a subquery. (Subqueries are discussed later in this chapter.)
2. You can select individual columns to form subgroups.

Summarizing several groups of rows

If you want to know the average salary of the employees in each of several stores, you could make separate AVG(sal) queries for each store. However, you could get the same information with one query by using the GROUP BY clause.

The GROUP BY clause divides a table into groups of rows where the rows in each group have the same value in a specified column. For example, to obtain the average salary in each of several stores, you would enter:

```
SELECT      storeno, AVG(sal)
FROM        Emp
GROUP BY    storeno;
```

This would return a listing of each store number and the average salary at each store. This example does not contain a WHERE clause, therefore the GROUP BY clause is placed after the FROM clause. If your query contains a WHERE clause, the GROUP BY clause would come after the WHERE clause.

You can also divide the rows of a table into groups based on values in more than one column. You might want to group all employees by store number and title. Do this by specifying both store number and title in the SELECT list and in the GROUP BY clause.

Putting a group function in a subquery

Suppose you want to find out which of several stores in the group made the greatest profit. You cannot enter SELECT sname, MAX(profit) because sname has a value for each row selected, while MAX(profit) has a single value for the whole query. But you can get this information with a subquery. It will look like this:

```
SELECT      sname, city, profit
FROM        Stores
WHERE       profit =
            (SELECT MAX(profit)
            FROM      Stores);
```

Miscellaneous functions

The miscellaneous functions are GREATEST, LEAST, and NVL. Their uses are explained in the following sections.

GREATEST

You can perform certain calculations with functions. GREATEST is a function with two or more arguments. The arguments are value names separated by commas. When GREATEST is evaluated by ORACLE, its value is the largest of its argument values.

All expressions after the first are converted to the type of the first before the comparison is done. The syntax is:

```
SELECT   <column_name>, GREATEST (<argument1>,
         <argument2>)
FROM     <tablename>;
```

For example, you might want to know which job title commands the higher income regardless of whether that income is from salary or commissions. To find out you could enter the following query:

```
SELECT   title, GREATEST (sal, comm)
FROM     Employees;
```

GREATEST can return any type of value. The type of value returned is the same as the type of value of the first argument. When GREATEST is applied to date values, a later date is considered greater than an earlier one. When applied to CHAR values, the greater value is the one that comes later in alphabetic order.

LEAST

The function LEAST works in exactly the same way as GREATEST except that it returns the smallest value of its argument values. Like GREATEST, it can return any type of CHAR, date or numeric value depending on the type of value of its first argument.

NULL value function (NVL)

The NULL value function (NVL) substitutes a value for nulls. Sometimes you might want to treat null values as zero (or some other number). For example, if your company employs people who receive commissions, then a null commission should perhaps be treated the same as a zero commission. On the other hand, if you find a null value in a column listing Social Security Numbers, it would not be appropriate to convert this to a zero.

You can use the NVL to convert a null value to a specified non-null value for the purpose of evaluating an expression.

NVL requires two arguments: an expression and a non-null value. Whenever NVL is evaluated, it will return the value of the expression if that value is non-null. If the value of the expression is null, then it will return the value of the second argument—the non-null value. The syntax is:

```
NVL(x,expr)
```

For example, if you want commissions treated as zero (0) whenever they are left blank, use the NVL function as follows:

```
NVL(comm,0)
```

Then, if you want to list the total income for each employee at store

No. 5, enter:

```
SELECT ename, sal + NVL(comm,0)
FROM Employees
WHERE storeno = 5;
```

NVL is especially important for use with group functions such as AVG and SUM, where ORACLE will automatically ignore, or count as zero, any null values in the data unless you specify otherwise by means of NVL. NVL can return a CHAR or DATE value as well as a number value, and the same two arguments as above apply.

Aliases

While aliases have many potential uses, the principal uses of substitute names for tables and columns are to:

- make a cryptic column name more meaningful when displayed
- abbreviate an often-used table or column name
- make a complicated SQL statement clearer
- distinguish between two appearances of the same column name or table name in any one SELECT statement

In addition, table and column aliases may be used whenever it is convenient to do so. The last purpose listed above usually involves a join of a table with itself, and therefore is considered in chapter 10, which is devoted exclusively to joins.

Column aliases

To create a column alias, enter the alias after the column name in the SELECT statement. For example, to make the computed column AVG(SAL) more meaningful when displayed, (for example in a report), enter:

```
SELECT      title, AVG(SAL) 'Average Salary'
FROM        Employees
GROUP BY    title
HAVING      AVG(SAL) >
            (SELECT AVG(SAL)
            FROM   Employees
            WHERE  title = 'secretary');
```

This query will list the AVG(SAL) of all employee titles where that average is greater than the average for secretaries, and the column heading will be "Average Salary" rather than AVG(SAL). Note that the column alias is only referred to in the SELECT statement. It is enclosed in single quotes because it consists of two words which are to be shown together over the displayed results. If the column alias were a single word and contained no special characters, such as * or %, the single quotes would not be necessary.

Table aliases

To create a table alias, define it in the FROM clause. The alias is then used as a qualifier in both the SELECT and WHERE clauses. For example, if you want to abbreviate the table name Salesmen to S, and the Customers table to C, in order to combine certain salesmen with customers, enter:

```
SELECT   S.*, C.*
FROM     Salesmen S, Customers C
WHERE    S.district = C.district;
AND      S.commission > 3000;
```

The use of the qualifying S. in the AND clause is not absolutely necessary, because only the Salesmen table contains a "commission." However, it is never wrong to use the complete specification whether or not an alias is being used.

Subqueries (subselects or nested selects)

A subquery (sometimes called a subselect or nested select) is a query contained in the WHERE clause of another query called the main query. The subquery will provide you with the results you need to complete the main query.

Subqueries are useful in building powerful, complex queries. They can always be broken down into two or more simple queries, but in most cases it is more efficient to use the subquery than the collection of simple queries. There is no limit in SQL to the number of subqueries that can be nested. However, such expressions can become so complex that it might be advisable to use a set of queries with fewer subqueries.

The syntax for a query containing a subquery is:

```
SELECT   <column1, column2, ..., columnN>
FROM     <tablename1>
WHERE    <column_i> IN
         (SELECT <column_j>
              FROM    <tablename2>
              WHERE   <condition>);
```

where column_i and column_j have the same datatype and width.

The subquery, or *inner query*, starts with the second SELECT statement, and is always surrounded with parentheses. The query starting with the first SELECT is called the *main query* or the *outer query*.

Theoretically, another subquery can be added after the second WHERE clause, and that same process repeated again and again. In practice however, too many subqueries can become confusing.

A subquery can refer to a different table from the one referred to by the main query, and you can use comparison operators other than IN to connect the query with the subquery.

You can use a subquery wherever you can use a WHERE clause, for example in the SELECT, UPDATE, INSERT, and DELETE commands.

You can use GROUP BY and HAVING clauses, but you cannot use ORDER BY or UNION clauses in a subquery.

As an example of a subquery, suppose you want to list all salesmen in your Employees Table whose commission is greater than $800. You can do so with the following command:

```
SELECT   employee_name, title, commission
FROM     Employees
WHERE    employee_name IN
         (SELECT employee_name
             FROM    Employees
             WHERE   commission > 800
             AND     title = 'salesman');
```

You could use the equal sign (=) in the first WHERE clause of the above query and omit the IN if you know ahead of time that only one row will be returned, as follows:

```
WHERE    employees =
         (SELECT  employee_name
         FROM     Employees
         WHERE    commission > 800
         AND      title = 'salesman');
```

However, if more than one row satisfies the subquery when the equal sign (=) is used, then SQL will return an error. If no rows satisfy the subquery and the equal sign (=) is used in the first WHERE clause, then SQL will return a NULL. Obviously, if you don't know how many rows will be returned, it is safer to use IN than the equal sign (=).

Subqueries that select more than one column

You also can use a subquery to select more than one column. In this case, put parentheses around the list of columns on the left side of the comparison operator. For example, if you want to find the suppliers who sell the same part at the same price as Acme, you would enter:

```
SELECT   supplier_name, part_name, price
FROM     Suppliers
WHERE    (part_name, price) IN
         (SELECT part_name, price
         FROM    Suppliers
         WHERE   supplier name = 'Acme');
```

You can combine a number of conditions in the WHERE clause by using AND and OR to connect these conditions in the subqueries. You may also use a subquery composed of two or more queries by using the operators AND, OR, and MINUS. These operators are useful when you construct subqueries referring to different tables. (Use of subqueries with the connectives mentioned in this paragraph is illustrated in the sections devoted specifically to those connectives.)

Subqueries using EXISTS

You can use a subquery with the EXISTS clause to test for existence. For example, for the query: List all customers for which there is a supplier in the same city, enter:

```
SELECT   customer_name
FROM     Customers
WHERE    EXISTS
         (SELECT city
         FROM Suppliers
         WHERE supplier.city = customer.city);
```

This query will return a list of all customers in a city where there is a supplier.

Subqueries using ANY or ALL

Some subqueries return only a single value; others can return more than one value. To have more than one value returned, use ANY or ALL between the comparison operator (=, =>, <=, <, >, or <>) and the subquery. For example, suppose you want to know which salesmen earn more commission than some salaried personnel. Your query must do two things: First, find the salaries of all personnel, and then select all commissions that are higher than the lowest salary. You can do this with the following query:

```
SELECT   employee-name
FROM     Employees
WHERE    title = 'salesman'
AND      commission > ANY
         (SELECT salary
         FROM   Employees
         WHERE title < > 'salesman');
```

If you use ALL after the comparison operator, the query will select those rows in which the commission is greater than all the values returned by the subquery. In other words, it will select salesmen whose commissions are higher than the highest salary of the non-salesman personnel. The query is:

```
SELECT   employee_name
FROM     Employees
WHERE    title = salesman
AND      commission > ALL
         (SELECT salary
         FROM    Employees
         WHERE   title < > salesman);
```

Correlated subqueries

In addition to the subqueries considered above (where each subquery was executed once, then the result used by the WHERE clause of the main query) you also can set up a subquery that gets executed repeatedly. This is called a *correlated subquery*. In a correlated subquery, it might be helpful to think in terms of a *candidate row*—a row that might, after certain operations are performed, fit the conditions of the query.

For example, suppose you want to find the suppliers whose price for a given part is higher than the average price for other suppliers of that product. You cannot pick out these suppliers simply by looking at the table of suppliers. The candidate rows are the suppliers whose prices will be compared to the average price for the part they supply. The evaluation proceeds like this:

1. Set up a main query to select the suppliers from the Suppliers table.
2. Set up a subquery to calculate the average price of each candidate supplier's part.

The main query will consider each candidate row. As it does so, it must invoke the subquery and tell it the supplier's part. Then the subquery must compute the average price for that supplier's part. Finally, the main query must compare the supplier's price to the average price for the part. This is called a *correlated subquery* because each execution of the subquery is correlated with the value of a field in one of the main query's candidate rows.

To set up the subquery, you need to use the letter X, or any other alias name, as a table alias. The alias (X) will appear in the main query and in the subquery; it refers to the value of a column in each candidate row. The complete query is as follows:

```
SELECT   name, part_name, price
FROM     Suppliers X
WHERE    price >
         (SELECT AVG (price)
         FROM    Suppliers
         WHERE   X.part_name = part_name);
```

Summary

The AND, OR, and MINUS connectives were discussed, and it was shown how IN and NOT IN could sometimes be substituted for these connectives. The SQL functions: character string, numeric string, date, aggregate, and miscellaneous were illustrated. The uses of aliases and subqueries were shown.

Chapter 6 exercises

Use the following tables to complete the exercises listed below:

Courses

Course Name	**Credit Hours**	**Semester**	**Staff**
Geography	3	Fall	Blane
Architecture	5	Summer	Smith
Trigonometry	3	Spring	Weeks
Planning	2	Spring	Jones
Psychology	3	Fall	Martin
Psychology	3	Spring	Gerber
Psychology	3	Fall	Gerber
Psychology	3	Spring	Martin
Biology	4	Fall	Gregory
Biology	4	Spring	Allen
Astronomy	5	Spring	Barnes
Biology	3	Summer	Allen
Algebra	2	Summer	Blane
Algebra	3	Fall	Weeks

Faculty

Name	**Rank**
Smith	Instructor
Gerber	Assistant professor
Weeks	Assistant professor
Allen	Instructor
Barnes	Professor
Blane	Instructor
Gregory	Assistant professor
Jones	Assistant professor
Martin	Assistant professor

Write the SQL statements for the following queries:

6.1 List the courses and credit hours of courses taught by Barnes in the Spring semester.

6.2 List the courses either taught by Barnes or offered in the Spring semester.

6.3 List the courses taught by either Barnes or Martin in the Fall semester.

6.4 Find the number of different instructors and the number of different ranks.

6.5 Determine the average number of credit hours taught by instructors.

6.6 Find all courses of four semester hours or less, taught in the Spring semester by an assistant professor.

6.7 Find all courses of at least three semester hours taught by someone other than Smith.

6.8 List the Fall courses and the faculty who teach them, with the faculty names shown alphabetically.

6.9 Determine the number of courses covered by the course list, and the number of different faculty members teaching.

6.10 List the Fall or Spring courses that are taught by assistant professors.

Answers to chapter 6 exercises

6.1
```
SELECT          course_name, credit_hours
FROM            Courses
WHERE           staff = 'Barnes'
AND             semester = 'spring';
```

6.2
```
SELECT          course_name
FROM            Courses
WHERE           staff = 'Barnes'
OR              semester = 'spring';
```

6.3
```
SELECT          course_name
FROM            Courses
WHERE           (staff = 'Barnes' OR staff =
                  'Martin')
AND             semester = 'fall';
```

It could also be entered as:

```
SELECT          course_name
FROM            Courses
WHERE           staff = 'Barnes'
AND             semester = 'fall'
UNION
SELECT          course_name
```

```
      FROM                      Courses
      WHERE                     staff = 'Martin'
      AND                       semester = 'fall';
```

6.4
```
SELECT COUNT (DISTINCT instructors),
COUNT (DISTINCT ranks)
FROM                      Faculty;
```

6.5
```
SELECT                    AVG(credit_hours)
FROM                      Courses
WHERE                     staff IN
                          (SELECT name
                          FROM    faculty
                          WHERE   rank = 'instructor');
```

6.6
```
SELECT                    course_name
FROM                      courses
WHERE                     credit_hours < = 4
AND                       semester = spring
AND                       staff IN
                          (SELECT name
                          FROM    Faculty
                          WHERE   rank = 'assist_prof');
```

6.7
```
SELECT                    course_name
FROM                      Courses
WHERE                     NOT staff = 'Smith'
AND                       credit_hours > = 3;
```

6.8
```
SELECT                    course_name, staff
FROM                      Courses
WHERE                     semester = 'fall'
ORDER BY                  staff;
```

6.9
```
SELECT COUNT(*), COUNT (DISTINCT staff)
FROM                      Courses;
```

6.10
```
SELECT                    course_name,
FROM                      Courses
WHERE                     (semester = spring OR semester = fall)
AND                       staff IN
(SELECT                   staff
FROM                      faculty
WHERE                     rank = 'assist_prof');
```

7

CHAPTER

Using data definition statements

In this chapter you will learn how to use ORACLE SQL commands to set up a small database, and in succeeding chapters, enlarge upon and extend its capabilities. The procedures will apply to a database of any size. The development will illustrate the use of SQL from the standpoint of a one-service (or product), single-user system on through a multi-user database management system for a multi-product, multi-service organization.

The design of the database, an important topic in its own right, will not be considered here because employment of the SQL commands will be the same regardless of how the system is designed. This text will assume that an appropriate design has been worked out for the situation at hand.

CREATE DATABASE

The database, which will consist of tables, must be created before you can put any tables in it or access it in any way. This involves several preliminary steps that are slightly different depending on your operating system and the version of ORACLE that you are using. On some systems, the database files are created automatically, and on some the DBA must manually create or allocate these files. Because these steps are independent of the use of SQL, they will not be fully discussed here, except to note that starting with ORACLE version 6, the database is created through the SQL*DBA utility. See your *SQL*Plus Database Administrator's Guide* for further details on opening, closing, mounting, and dismounting a database.

Let's assume that you have successfully logged onto the system, you have checked the INIT.ORA file, and performed the other preliminary operations that result in your ORACLE database being mounted and open.

A complete relational database system may consist of many databases, with some limitation on the number. Therefore, each database created must have a name. Let's name this one "Service Co.," abbreviated to serv_co, by entering:

```
CREATE DATABASE serv_co;
```

The CREATE DATABASE command sets up a set of system tables to hold information about the database. Because you are creating a small database in this example, it will be sufficient to use the defaults for the arguments in the syntax of the CREATE DATABASE statement shown in chapter 4. Because all the arguments are optional, failing to specify them results in the default values.

You are now ready to designate storage areas and to enroll users.

CREATE TABLESPACE

ORACLE uses the CREATE TABLESPACE command to set aside a storage area for a database. One tablespace, SYSTEM, is created automatically when the database is created. The following command will create an additional tablespace with one physical datafile. Keep in mind that the default tablespace storage is operating-system specific and that what appears here is merely an example. Check your operating systems manual and remember only a DBA can create a tablespace.

```
CREATE TABLESPACE SPACE_2
DATAFILE 'SPACE_FILE2.DAT' SIZE 20 M
    DEFAULT STORAGE (INITIAL 10K NEXT 50K
    MINEXTENTS 1 MAXEXTENTS NULL
    PCTINCREASE 10)
```

```
ONLINE;
```

The default, ONLINE, means that the tablespace will be available immediately for users who have been granted access to it. The storage parameters are operating system specific. See your operating system manual for details.

CREATE ROLLBACK SEGMENT

You should create at least one rollback segment for each tablespace created. Only a DBA or a user who has been granted RESOURCE privilege on the named tablespace can create a rollback segment:

```
CREATE PUBLIC ROLLBACK SEGMENT RBS_2
TABLESPACE SPACE-2
STORAGE    (INITIAL 50000
            INCREMENT 50000
            MAXEXTENTS 10);
```

You can only create a rollback segment for a tablespace when the tablespace is online. You can have multiple rollback segments on any one tablespace. Multiple rollback segments will usually improve performance. See the ORACLE *Database Administrator's Guide* for details on the optimal number and size of rollback segments.

CREATE TABLE

Because a relational database consists of tables, and from the user's viewpoint, nothing but tables, your most frequent task is creating those tables. Operating system or user-interface pathways to create and/or access tables will not be discussed in this text. However, the construction of more complex SQL statements that will optimize existing search routes will be discussed in chapter 11.

A base table is defined and created with the following syntax:

```
CREATE TABLE <tablename>
    (<column definition(s)>
    [UNIQUE constraint]
    [NOT NULL constraint]
    [<DEFAULT clause>]
    [<referential constraint definition>]
    [CHECK <constraint definition>]);
```

where the <column definition> contains each column name along with the datatype and data size for that column, and the constraint definitions.

If UNIQUE is specified, then that column cannot contain any duplicate values.

If NOT NULL is specified, then a value other than NULL must be filled in for every insertion in that column. If UNIQUE is specified for any column, then NOT NULL must also be specified for that column.

If both UNIQUE and NOT NULL are specified, these two constraints on a column make the column eligible for use as a primary key, which is discussed in chapter 11.

If UNIQUE is specified, then PRIMARY KEY can be specified for that column.

If DEFAULT is specified, it must tell what to insert in a column if an insertion doesn't specify a value for that column.

If there is a <referential constraint>, then the reference specification must specify a column name (or names) and indicate that it is a foreign key in a named reference table.

If a CHECK constraint definition is specified, then a column will be referenced and a search condition specified—which cannot contain a subquery, a set function specification or a target specification.

For purposes of illustrating the SQL syntax in this and succeeding chapters, let's assume you are working with a company whose initial function is to sell automobile replacement parts. The company has four employees: the owner, a secretary, and two salesmen. Your job is to work with the owner to transform his paper files to a relational database management system using SQL as its query language.

The company buys the parts in quantity from each manufacturer, and resells them individually to automobile repair shops. Let's say you have determined that you'll need the following:

1. A table containing the names and addresses of the part suppliers, the part numbers and part names of the items they supply, and the price of those parts.
2. A table containing the names and addresses of repair shops (customers) and listing what they have ordered, what they owe, and the due date of their payments.
3. A list of personnel, their Social Security numbers, their addresses, their salaries, any commissions paid to them, and their job titles.

These three tables will get you started; when you need more tables, or more columns in these tables, the relational form of the database will allow you to make additions at any time without disrupting the operation or compromising the database.

The syntax shown in chapter 4 for creating any table is:

```
CREATE TABLE <tablename>
     (<column1_name>        <datatype>, <datasize>
      <column2_name>        <datatype>, <datasize>
```

```
...
<columnN-name>          <datatype>, <datasize>);
```

The datatype of each column must be specified in the CREATE TABLE statement. The types of data supported by ORACLE SQL are shown in Table 3-1.

Therefore, let's set up the first table as follows:

```
CREATE TABLE Suppliers
    (Name          CHAR(30) NOT NULL
    Address        CHAR(30) NOT NULL
    Part_no        CHAR(12) UNIQUE NOT NULL
    Part_name      CHAR(15)
    Price          NUM(11));
```

This will result in a table where 30 CHAR spaces are allowed for the supplier's name, 30 CHAR spaces for the supplier's address, 12 CHAR spaces for recording the supplier's part number, 15 CHAR spaces for the part name and 11 numerical spaces for the price of the part. (CHAR spaces are used for the part number because these numbers are merely labels and cannot be used with arithmetic operations. Using CHAR will allow you to record any letters that might accompany the numbers of some parts.)

Notice that the NOT NULL constraint on the Name column and on the Address column ensures that if a supplier's name is entered, the address must also be entered, and vice versa. The UNIQUE NOT NULL specification on the Part_no column ensures not only that this column will not be left blank, it also prevents any duplication of part numbers. (Therefore, Part_no could serve as a primary key.) However, this constraint means that if two suppliers happen to use the same number for one of their parts, the second number will be rejected because duplicates will not be allowed. In that case, you could add the suppliers ID to each part number to distinguish them.

The part name and the price do not have to be entered when name, address, and part number are entered because there is no NOT NULL specification on those columns.

The table just described will be too wide to fit on the 80-column screen of most CRT's without reducing the size of the characters. Therefore, it will not be possible to see the whole table at once; it will have to be scrolled horizontally which might become inconvenient when entering orders. For the moment let's let this problem stand, and consider it in an exercise at the end of the chapter.

Now, you must set up the table listing the customers:

```
CREATE TABLE Customers
    (Name          CHAR(30)NOT NULL
    Address        CHAR(30)NOT NULL
```

```
        Part_no         CHAR(12)
        Part_Name       CHAR(15)
        Price           NUM(10)
        Due_Date        NUM(10));
```

As with the Supplier table, this table will contain a Name column with a maximum CHAR width of 30 spaces, Customer Address column with a CHAR width of 30 spaces, a Part No. column with a CHAR width of 12 spaces, a Part Name column with a CHAR width of 15 spaces, a Price column with a numerical width of 10 spaces, and a Due Date column with a Numerical width of 10 spaces.

The NOT NULL constraint on the Customer name and Address columns specifies that those columns cannot be left blank. Therefore, if any item in a row is filled in, the Customer name and Address columns also must be filled in.

Again, there is the problem of a table that extends so far horizontally that it will be necessary for the user to scroll over to see it all. This brings with it the same problem as the Suppliers table. Again, let's leave this problem to be resolved in the exercises at the end of the chapter.

The few employees of this company would hardly need a table were it not for the need to file periodic government reports on amounts paid to them. Also, an employee might leave during the year and be replaced by another employee. Therefore, at the end of any year, the employee table might contain several more names than the number actually working at the company on that date. These year-end reports must include everyone employed during the year whether or not they are still on the payroll. The table must allow for this. Therefore, let's set it up as follows:

```
CREATE TABLE Employees
      (Name         CHAR(50)
      Address       CHAR(50)
      SS_no         CHAR(12) UNIQUE NOT NULL
      Title         CHAR(10)
      Salary        NUM(8)
      Commission    NUM(8));
```

The UNIQUE NOT NULL constraint on the SS_no column will prevent the entry of the same Social Security number for two different employees as well as ensuring that this column is never NULL. Note that SS_no is a CHAR datatype. This will allow a dash (-) to be inserted as is conventionally done with Social Security numbers, for example 000-00-0000. If the numbers are to be used without inserting the dashes, then a NUM datatype can be used.

No two columns in the same table can have the same name although two columns in different tables may have the same name. The table's name may be preceded by the ID of the person who created the table. This is the name the person uses in logging onto the database. When an ID is used, it is separated from the table name by a period (.), for example:

```
CREATE TABLE barber.employees
```

would create an Employees table owned by the user whose ID is Barber.

Sometimes it might be necessary to move a set of data from an existing table to another table that has been set up for some special purpose. In this case it is possible to set up the new table, and transfer the desired set of data all with one command. The syntax for doing this is:

```
CREATE TABLE <new_tablename> [<column1, column2, ... columnN>]
AS      SELECT    <column1, column2, ... columnN>)
        FROM      <old_tablename>
        WHERE     <condition>;
```

The SQL statement following the word AS is a subquery designating the information to be taken from the existing table. You do not need to specify datatypes or sizes for the new table because these will be determined by the datatypes and sizes of the columns in the old table.

For example, you might want a special confidential list of the customers who have not paid their bill within 60 days after the due date, so that these names can be turned over to a collection agency. To set up this new table, which for this example call Deadbeats, and put the non-paying customers accounts into it, enter:

```
CREATE TABLE Deadbeats (name, address, amount, due_date)
AS      SELECT    name, address, amount, due-date
        FROM      Customers
        WHERE     due_date >= current - 60;
```

Note the use of the value expression minus (−) in the WHERE clause of the subquery. The form for setting up dates in such a way that arithmetic operations can be performed on them is called a Julian date. ORACLE provides for converting date data into Julian dates. See your *Database Administrator's Guide* provided by Oracle Corporation, for this conversion.

The above command will set up the new table Deadbeats, and copy into it all rows in the Customers table where the account is 60 or more days overdue. This command does not remove the specified rows from the Customers table. To remove them you must enter a DELETE command as explained in chapter 8.

CREATE SYNONYM

You can use the CREATE SYNONYM command to create a synonym for a table or view to reduce the amount of typing necessary to refer to a frequently used table or view. Do this for the Customer's table, using the letter C as the synonym, by entering the following:

```
CREATE PUBLIC SYNONYM C
FOR Customers;
```

Using the optional word PUBLIC in this statement indicates that you are creating a synonym that any user can use.

CREATE DATABASE LINK

Use the CREATE DATABASE LINK command to link a user on a remote database to the local database. The remote can be either a remote ORACLE or some other remote database, such as an IBM DB2. To do this, you must have access to an ORACLE user name on the remote database, and SQL*Net must be installed on both the local and remote databases.

For example, using the syntax shown in chapter 4, you can define a database link named Denver referring to user Burkhart with password NEVER on database D:DENVER-PDQ, by entering:

```
CREATE DATABASE LINK DENVER
CONNECT TO BURKHART IDENTIFIED BY NEVER
USING 'D:DENVER-PDQ';
```

Once this command is executed, you can enter SELECT statements on tables owned by Burkhart. To do so, you must add @<linkname> to the FROM clause. For example, if you want to query the Employee table (synonym EMP), which is owned by Burkhart, you should enter:

```
SELECT * FROM EMP@DENVER;
```

This link that you have created also allows you to query tables in the Denver database which Burkhart does not own, but to which he has access. It will first connect to user Burkhart, and then query the desired table. For example, if Burkhart has access to the Clients table, owned by Smith, you can access the Clients table by entering:

```
SELECT * FROM SMITH.CLIENTS@DENVER:
```

CREATE VIEW

In creating a view, you use the same initial command as that used to create a table, but from there on, the process is slightly different for two reasons:

1. The columns are already set up in the table from which the view will be taken, therefore the column datatype and width in the view will be whatever they are in the base table, and do not need to be specified in the CREATE VIEW command.

2. To set up a view, you must SELECT the columns you want out of the base table(s). Selecting columns amounts to manipulating the data rather than defining it, and this operation comes under the rules for data manipulation as explained in chapter 4.

You might want to create a view of the Employees table that does not include salaries. To do so, name the view Employee History, and list all columns except the salary column in the SELECT statement as follows:

```
CREATE VIEW Emp__Hist
 AS      SELECT    name, address, SS__no
         FROM      Employees;
```

Suppose you wanted to create a view showing each salesman's customers, but you want to set it up so that when a salesman accesses that view, he only sees his own customers and not the customers of the other salesmen. To do so, you can name the view My Customers and set up the SELECT statement so that it will only yield the customers of the logged-in user at any one session. It will look like this:

```
CREATE VIEW My__Cust
 AS      SELECT    *
         FROM      Customers
         WHERE     ename = user
         AND       job = salesman;
```

In this case, user is called a *pseudo-column* because there is actually no column with that name, but the login ID will supply the identification.

With this view, each salesman will view only information about his own customers. Also, if a non-salesman happens to try to access this view, the query will fail because the WHERE clause—ename = user AND job = salesman—will not be satisfied.

There are many situations where creating a view will supply a simple answer to a problem.

CREATE INDEX

CREATE and DROP are the only SQL operations on indices available to an end user. These are all you will need because decisions about using specific indices for optimal retrieval paths should be made by the system rather than by the user. To create an index on the City column of the Customers table: give the name of the index (using the synonym C for the table name); identify the table; and (in parentheses) list the column(s) containing the information to go in the index as follows:

```
CREATE INDEX C__city
ON C (city);
```

ALTER TABLE

A relational database can be easily altered to accommodate the changing needs of a database over time. In this context the ALTER TABLE command provides one way to make changes. In ORACLE SQL this command has two forms:

```
ALTER TABLE...ADD
```

and

```
ALTER TABLE...MODIFY
```

These two ALTER commands can be used to add a new column to an existing table; to increase or decrease a column size; to change the datatype of a column; to add a NOT NULL specification to a column; and to remove a NOT NULL specification from a column.

Altering a table only changes the current and future versions of the table. It does not change what is already in the database. Rules covering the use of ALTER TABLE commands ensure that their use does not compromise the integrity of the database. Therefore, in making the changes listed in the previous paragraph, the SQL command ALTER TABLE can be used only as follows.

To add a column to the existing columns in a table The SQL command for adding a column is ALTER TABLE followed by the name of the table you want to alter, and the command ADD followed by the column name where the change is to take place, and the desired change.

When you add a column, this new column will be placed to the right of the existing columns. All fields in the new column are initially NULL, but you cannot specify NOT NULL when adding a new column if your table already has some rows in it. There is a way, however, to add a NOT NULL specification to a table with existing rows, which is explained in a later section.

Suppose you decide that the Customer Table should contain telephone numbers. You can add a column to contain these by entering:

```
ALTER TABLE Customers
    ADD phone_no (CHAR 15);
```

To increase the size of an existing column An existing base table can be altered at any time by increasing the column size, or by changing its number of decimal places. The SQL command is ALTER TABLE followed by the name of the table where the modification is to occur, the SQL command MODIFY, the column name to be modified, and then the desired modification.

Suppose that due to a planned expansion of the company's services, you are planning to add some new job titles. The existing column size will not allow for this, therefore the column width needs to be expanded. To do this, enter:

```
ALTER TABLE Employees
    MODIFY (title CHAR (40));
```

This will enlarge the original title column to 40 spaces.

To decrease the size of an existing column, but only if all rows of that column have the value NULL Suppose you decide to enter all supplier names by a three-letter code instead of by their full names. This will allow you to decrease the width of the name column in your Supplier table. Do so by entering:

```
ALTER TABLE Suppliers
    MODIFY (name CHAR(3));
```

To change the datatype of an existing column, but only if all rows of that column have the value NULL at the time the datatype is changed Suppose you realize that the due-date column in the Customers table has been entered as NUM when it would be more convenient as a DATE datatype. If you have not yet made any entries in that column, you may make the change with the following statement:

```
ALTER TABLE Customers
    MODIFY due_date (date)(10);
```

To assign the NOT NULL constraint to a column The NOT NULL specification can only be used with the ALTER TABLE command if the column being altered contains no NULL entries.

At this point, all customer phone numbers have been entered into the Customer table with no NULLs. To be sure that this practice is followed in the future, you decide to put a NOT NULL constraint on that column. Do so by entering:

```
ALTER TABLE Customers
    MODIFY (phone_no CHAR(15)) NOT NULL;
```

Obviously this restriction on the ALTER TABLE is to avoid destroying the integrity of the database by setting up a NOT NULL column where some rows have already been filled in with NULL values.

To remove the NOT NULL constraint from a column A column can be changed from NOT NULL to include NULL values with the ALTER TABLE command. You can change a column from NOT NULL to NULL by adding the NULL clause to the column specification. Suppose that the NOT NULL constraint on the Social Security number column in the Employees table is causing a delay in entering the names of new employees. You decide to drop that constraint by entering:

```
ALTER TABLE Employees
    MODIFY ((SS_no CHAR) NULL);
```

You cannot use the ALTER command to change a synonym. If you want to change a synonym, you must use the DROP SYNONYM command, then the CREATE command to create a new synonym. Note that there is no ALTER VIEW command in SQL.

DROP commands

This section discusses the DROP commands in ORACLE SQL.

DROP DATABASE Dropping a database will drop all of the tables, views and indices defined on that database. Therefore, you should only drop a database after considering the total effects of doing so.

DROP TABLESPACE You cannot drop the SYSTEM tablespace. To drop any other tablespace, you must have DBA privilege. The DROP TABLESPACE command is set up to keep you from inadvertently dropping a tablespace containing database objects. The command is:

```
DROP TABLESPACE <tablespace> [INCLUDING CONTENTS];
```

The optional term [INCLUDING CONTENTS] must be used if you are dropping a tablespace with database objects in it. In other words, you can drop an empty tablespace without the optional term, but if the tablespace has contents, ORACLE requires that you make it clear that you know you are dropping these contents by adding [INCLUDING CONTENTS] to the command.

You cannot drop a tablespace while users are accessing its data, index, rollback or temporary segments. Therefore, you should take the tablespace offline before attempting to drop it. To drop a tablespace called Deadbeats, enter:

```
DROP TABLESPACE Deadbeats INCLUDING CONTENTS;
```

DROP CLUSTER To drop a cluster, you must own it or have DBA privilege. The general form is:

```
DROP CLUSTER [user.]cluster [INCLUDING TABLES]
```

When you drop a cluster, you also drop the cluster index and you return all cluster space, including index blocks, to the appropriate tablespace(s).

The DROP CLUSTER command is set up in such a way that you cannot inadvertently drop a cluster with tables in it. The term [INCLUDING TABLES] is only optional if the cluster does not contain any tables. If you attempt to drop a cluster containing tables, you must add the term [INCLUDING TABLES]. To drop a cluster containing the Deadbeats Table(s), enter:

```
DROP CLUSTER Deadbeats INCLUDING TABLES;
```

DROP TABLE To remove a table from the database, use the DROP TABLE command followed by the name of the table, as follows:

```
DROP TABLE Deadbeats;
```

Dropping a table drops all views defined on that table. It will also drop any indices defined on that table. Therefore, the DROP TABLE command should only be used after consideration of its effect on the rest of the database.

DROP SYNONYM To drop a synonym you must own the synonym and/or have the necessary privilege to drop it. As noted previously, if you want to change a synonym, you cannot do it with the ALTER command. You must use the DROP SYNONYM command, then use the CREATE SYNONYM command to create the new synonym.

DROP VIEW You can use the drop command to drop views as well as tables. Dropping a view does not drop the table from which the view was derived, but it does drop the view from the index.

DROP INDEX To drop an index, use the DROP INDEX command followed by the name of the index. Because it is possible to have two indices with the same name on different tables, it is safest to specify the name of the table for which the index is being dropped. For example, you might have an index on the phone number column in your Employees table, as well as on the phone number column in your Customer table. To make clear that you are only dropping the index on phone numbers in your Employees table, use the table name in your DROP command, as follows:

```
DROP INDEX phone_no
ON Employees;
```

Dropping an index does not drop the tables or views on which the index is based, but dropping an index might affect the access paths by which information can be retrieved by the system. Therefore, you should consider the effect on optimum use of the database before dropping an index.

Summary

This chapter illustrates the use of the Data Definition Statements CREATE DATABASE, CREATE TABLESPACE, CREATE TABLE, CREATE SYNONYM, CREATE VIEW, CREATE INDEX, ALTER TABLE, DROP DATABASE, DROP TABLESPACE, DROP TABLE, DROP VIEW, and DROP INDEX. It sets up a fictional situation to show the use of these terms in setting up a database.

Chapter 7 exercises

7.1 Suggest a solution to the problem posed in the first section of this chapter regarding the horizontal size of the Supplier table and the Customer table.

7.2 Set up a table of prospective customers, called Prospects, containing customer names, addresses, phone numbers where available, and the salesman assigned to them.

7.3 What is the purpose of the stipulation that a column must contain only NULL values if the ALTER...MODIFY command is used to decrease the column size?

7.4 What is the purpose of the stipulation that a column must have no entries in it if the NOT NULL specification is added with the ALTER ...MODIFY command?

7.5 Increase the width of the Part_no column in the Customer table and change it to the numerical datatype.

7.6a Make up a table called "Wimbleton" of customers who live in that area, and put those customers' names and addresses in it all with one command.

7.6b What would be the advantage of creating a view Wimbleton rather than a table?

7.7 Add a column to the table you made up in exercise 7.6, to show the telephone numbers of the Wimbleton customers.

7.8 Remove the Deadbeats table from the database.

7.9 Enlarge the name column in the Customers table to a character string of length 40.

7.10 Write a command to make certain that no user in the company will leave the due date blank in the Customers table.

Answers to chapter 7 exercises

7.1 Create a view for each showing only those columns needed for specific purposes.

7.2
```
CREATE TABLE prospects
          (name        CHAR(30)UNIQUE NOT NULL
          address      CHAR(35)
          phone        CHAR(12)
          salesman     CHAR(20));
```

7.3 Values already in the table may exceed the reduced column size.

7.4 A row with a NULL value entry may already exist in that column.

7.5
```
ALTER TABLE customers
MODIFY part_no (NUM)(20);
```

7.6a
```
CREATE TABLE wimbleton
        AS      SELECT      name, address
                FROM        customers
                WHERE       address = 'Wimbleton';
```

7.6b A view would reflect future changes in the Customers table, such as updates, whereas a separate table would not.

7.7
```
ALTER TABLE wimbleton
ADD phone CHAR(12);
```

7.8
```
DROP TABLE deadbeats;
```

7.9
```
ALTER TABLE customers
MODIFY     (name)(CHAR)(40);
```

7.10
```
ALTER TABLE customers
MODIFY     (due_date) NOT NULL;
```

8

CHAPTER

Using data manipulation statements

As soon as the base tables are set up, you can begin inserting data into the database, updating it, changing it, deleting it, and querying it. All of these operations come under the general class of data manipulation.

This chapter will explain and illustrate the basic data manipulation commands. Later chapters will show how these commands can be used in conjunction with other SQL statements to query the database, to optimize retrieval, and to perform more complicated operations.

The data manipulation commands discussed in this chapter are:

INSERT

UPDATE

DELETE

SELECT
CREATE VIEW

INSERT

The INSERT command is used to put rows, or parts of rows, into tables. There are two commonly used general forms:

(1)
```
INSERT
INTO      <tablename> (<column1_name, column2_name, ...>)
VALUES    (<value1, value2, ...>);
```

The above form is used when you insert a single row or part of a single row.

(2)
```
INSERT
INTO      <tablename> (<column1_name, column2_name, ...>)
          (<subquery>);
```

In this second form, the result of evaluating the subquery is inserted into the listed columns of the named table. This form is usually used when multiple rows are being inserted. Examples are shown later in this chapter.

Any value inserted must match the datatype of the column into which the insertion is being made. Character values inserted must be enclosed in single quotes. NULL and numerical values should not be enclosed in quotes.

Inserting part or all of a single row

If values are being inserted into all columns in the table, then column names do not have to be listed after the table name. However, the column values being inserted must appear in the same order as the order of the column names when the table was created, with no omitted values. In this case, the syntax is:

```
INSERT
INTO    <tablename>
VALUES  (<value1, value2, value3, ...>);
```

For example, to insert the secretary, Ms. Barber, into the Employee table created in chapter 7, filling in all columns in the table, the command would be:

```
INSERT
INTO    Employees
VALUES  ('Barber', 'Ourtown', '000-21-9990', 'Sec', 900);
```

This command inserts a row that stores the following information: Barber, whose address is Ourtown, Social Security Number 000-21-9990, whose title is Secretary, and whose salary is $900.

If you are inserting fewer column values than the number of columns in the table, then you must either specify column names, or insert a NULL value for the column where you are not making an insert—given, that column does not contain a NOT NULL specification. In this case, the syntax is:

```
INSERT
INTO     <tablename> (<column1_name, column3_name>)
VALUES   (<value1, value3>);
```

or

```
INSERT
INTO     <tablename>
VALUES   (<value1, NULL, value3>);
```

For example, you can insert some of the information for one of the salesmen, Charles, even though you do not know his address or salary at this time:

```
INSERT      Name, SS_no, Title
INTO        Employees
VALUES      ('Charles', '000-31-9999', 'Salesman');
```

This statement specifies, after INSERT, the columns that are to be filled. The other method is shown in the statement below:

```
INSERT
INTO        Employees
VALUES      ('Charles', NULL, '000-31-9999', 'Salesman',
                NULL,);
```

In this statement no columns are specified after INSERT, but all columns are accounted for—in the order in which they were originally placed in the table—after VALUES, and they are represented either by a specific value or by a NULL.

Both of these entries indicate that you know Charles' name, but not his address; you know his Social Security Number (if you did not know his Social Security Number you could not make any entry for him because you cannot insert a NULL value for Social Security Number) and his title, but you do not know his salary.

If one column in a table contains a NOT NULL specification, then you cannot fill in any of the columns in that table until you have a value for the NOT NULL column. However, you may fill in one or more of the other columns with NULL.

For example, the company has just agreed to work with Acme, a new supplier in Chicago, but you do not yet know the part number Acme assigns to its carburetors although you know the price is $150. Let's insert the information you have into the Suppliers table:

```
INSERT
INTO        suppliers
VALUES      ('Acme', 'Chicago', NULL, 150);
```

This will leave the part number blank, while filling in the other three columns.

If you specify values for some columns, but do not mention the other columns in a row, then SQL will assume that every column is to be filled with a value, and will insert NULLs in any columns that you did not list—unless that column has a NOT NULL specification. If the column has a NOT NULL specification, and you didn't list that column, the entry will be rejected.

In the previous Acme example, you could have omitted the NULL value and SQL would have filled it in if you had specified the columns for which you are supplying values, as in the following:

```
INSERT
INTO        Suppliers (name, address, price)
VALUES      ('Acme', 'Chicago', 150);
```

It should be pointed out that omitting column names in the INSERT statement can cause problems if the number or order of the column names has changed since they were listed in the original CREATE TABLE statement. For example, if a column that once allowed a NULL value has been altered in the meantime and a NOT NULL specification added, the entry might be rejected. Assuming that the number and order of column names has remained constant is especially risky within an application program.

Inserting multiple rows or parts of multiple rows

The multiple row INSERT statement shown in the "INSERT" section can be used to select information already in one table and insert it into another table.

For example, if you are no longer doing business with Chicago suppliers, and want to pull them out of the current Suppliers table yet retain their records, you can create a new table called Former Suppliers, and put the Chicago suppliers in it. This can be done with the following commands:

```
CREATE TABLE Former_suppliers
        (name,      CHAR(10)
        part_no     NUM(5)
        price       NUM(10));
```

and

```
INSERT
INTO        Former_suppliers (name, part_no, price)
```

```
SELECT   name, part_no, price
FROM     Suppliers
WHERE    city = 'Chicago';
```

The result of the INSERT command will be entered into the new table Former Suppliers. The above does not remove the Chicago suppliers from the current Suppliers Table however, it merely copies their records into the Former Suppliers Table. To remove the Chicago suppliers from the current Suppliers table, you must use the DELETE command illustrated later in this chapter.

UPDATE

The UPDATE command is used to change values in existing rows. The general form is:

```
UPDATE    <tablename>
SET       <column1 = newvalue1>,
          <column2 = newvalue2>,
          <column3 = newvalue3>
[WHERE    <condition>];
```

When you use the SET clause with the UPDATE command, it must indicate which columns are to be updated and what will be the new values in those columns. It is used to impose a condition on all rows specified in the WHERE clause. This avoids having to update each row individually. For example, let's give the secretary a raise from $900 to $1000 and change her title to administrative assistant. The command to do this will be:

```
UPDATE    Employees
SET       title = adm_asst,
          salary = 1000
WHERE     name = 'Barber';
```

The UPDATE command affects all the rows that meet the condition stated in the WHERE clause. If the WHERE clause is omitted, all rows will be updated. For example, if the above update contained only the following:

```
UPDATE    Employees
SET       Title = 'adm_asst',
          Salary = 1000;
```

then every employee listed in the Employees table would have his or her title changed to administrative assistant, and his/her salary changed to $1000 regardless of what values these columns had before the update.

You can update several rows at once by specifying conditions in the WHERE clause that will apply to those rows.

As just shown in the general form of the UPDATE command, you can update several columns in each row with a single UPDATE command by listing those columns after the word SET. For example, suppose you wanted to give all salesmen listed in the Employees table a 10 percent raise. You can do this with one command as follows:

```
UPDATE    Employees
SET       salary = 1.1 * salary
WHERE     title = 'salesman';
```

The WHERE clause in an UPDATE command may contain a subquery. For example:

```
UPDATE    <tablename>
SET       salary = 1.1 * salary
WHERE     commission =
          (subquery);
```

Using a subquery in the WHERE clause, as shown here, will allow you to get the information for the update, and then to make the update all with one command.

DELETE

To remove rows from a table, use the DELETE command. The syntax is as follows:

```
DELETE
FROM <tablename>
[WHERE <condition>];
```

You cannot delete partial rows, therefore it is not necessary to include the column names. The condition stated in the WHERE clause will determine which rows are deleted.

To delete one row from a table, specify a condition in the WHERE clause applying to just that row.

To delete several rows from a table (all with one command) specify the condition common to all of the rows.

To delete all the rows from a table (all with one command) omit the WHERE clause and enter only the command:

```
DELETE FROM <tablename>;
```

For example, suppose that all of the names in your Deadbeats table have now been turned over to a bill collector, and you have no delinquent customers at this time. Then you might want to clear the Deadbeat table, but leave it in the database so you can use it again if necessary. To do this, enter:

```
DELETE FROM Deadbeats;
```

This command will remove all of the rows from the table, leaving only the column specifications and table name. Note that this differs from the DROP command which would remove the table name and column specifications, as well as all rows.

SELECT

To query the database and retrieve information from it, use the SELECT command. The general form of the SELECT command is:

```
SELECT    <column1, column2, column3, ...>
FROM      <tablename>;
```

If there is more than one column specified after the SELECT command, these columns must be separated by a comma.

Columns are returned in the order specified in the SELECT statement, not in the order in which they were originally entered into the table when it was created.

If you want to see entries in all columns of a table, use the asterisk after the SELECT:

```
SELECT *
FROM   <tablename>;
```

This command retrieves all columns and all rows from the named table.

The SELECT command and the FROM clause are necessary for any SQL query. The SELECT command and the FROM clause must appear before any other clauses in a query.

To retrieve only a specified set of rows from all columns of a table, state the common characteristic of the rows you want in a WHERE clause:

```
SELECT *
FROM      <tablename>
WHERE     <condition>;
```

For example, to retrieve all of the information on only the suppliers located in Dallas from the Suppliers table, use the following command:

```
SELECT *
FROM      Suppliers
WHERE     city = 'Dallas';
```

You can specify any number of conditions to further delimit the set of rows you want to retrieve. For example, you might want to retrieve only those Dallas suppliers from whom you buy valves. You can do this by adding another condition to the WHERE clause:

```
SELECT *
FROM       Suppliers
WHERE      city = 'Dallas'
AND        part_name = 'valve';
```

Rows returned in response to a SELECT command are retrieved and displayed in an arbitrary order. If you want them returned in a specific order, then you must use the term ORDER BY, which is discussed in chapter 5. There are many forms and many uses of the SELECT statement. These appear in later chapters.

CREATE VIEW

Even though CREATE is a data definition command when used with CREATE TABLE and CREATE INDEX, the CREATE VIEW command is included in this list of data manipulation statements because it can only be completed by using the SELECT command.

You could set up a complicated query to select the information you want out of a large table, but it will usually be more convenient to create a view of the table showing only what you want. There are a number of advantages to creating a view. These and other special topics will be discussed in chapter 11, which emphasizes working with views.

The syntax for creating a view is:

```
CREATE VIEW <viewname> [(<view_column_names>)]
 AS     SELECT     <column1_name, column2_name, ...>
        FROM       <tablename>
        WHERE      <condition>;
```

The target list of view column names shown after the view name, is optional. For example, if you wanted to see only those suppliers who supply filters, you could do so by creating a view of them, as follows:

```
CREATE VIEW filter_suppliers
 AS     SELECT     name, address, part_no, price
        FROM       Suppliers
        WHERE      part_name = 'filters';
```

Note that the specification for the view is actually a SQL query. You may use any valid SQL query in a CREATE VIEW command, except that you cannot use an ORDER BY clause in a view. If you want the rows ordered in a specific way, you must do it with a separate query directed to the view after you have created it. The ordering of the rows retrieved from views is discussed in chapter 11.

To query a view, use a WHERE clause just as you would use it in querying a table:

```
SELECT    <column_name(s)>
FROM      <viewname>
WHERE     <condition(s)>;
```

If you change the information in the table underlying the view, the information in the view will also change. If you update the underlying table, the values in the view will also be updated.

If you insert or delete rows in the table underlying the view, these rows will also be added to or deleted from the view. See chapter 11 for further details on working with views.

Summary

This chapter shows how to use the data manipulation statements INSERT, UPDATE, DELETE, SELECT, and CREATE VIEW in maintaining and querying a database. It also introduces the concept of views and shows why they might be used instead of complete base tables.

Chapter 8 exercises

8.1 In the "INSERT" section, at the beginning of this chapter, the statement appears "If one column in a table contains a NOT NULL specification, then you cannot fill in any of the columns in that table until you have a value for the NOT NULL column." Is this statement simply a rule, or is there a logical reason behind it? If there is a logical reason, what is it?

8.2 Add a new employee named Carson, of Westville, Social Security Number 000-32-4341, whose salary has not yet been determined, to the Employees table.

8.3 An employee named Gray has left the company. Remove his name from the Employee table and put it in a new table of Former Employees.

8.4 A table called Applicants was set up to hold the names and phone numbers of persons responding to a job opening. Because Carson was hired for this position, the other applicants' names are no longer needed. Remove this table from the database.

8.5 Query the database for the name, address and Social Security Number of all the accountants now employed.

8.6 Set up a virtual table containing all information on all accountants now employed.

8.7 Give all accountants a five percent raise.

8.8 Give all employees a five percent raise.

8.9 The New York supplier named Alcoe has now moved to Atlanta. Change this information in the database.

8.10 Set up a view showing salesmen's names and salaries.

Answers to chapter 8 exercises

8.1 If you do not have a value for the NOT NULL column, then filling in any of the other columns in the table would leave the NOT NULL column as a NULL, which is not allowed by the NOT NULL specification.

8.2
```
INSERT
INTO        Employees
VALUES      ('Carson', 'Westville', '000-32-4341', NULL);
```

8.3
```
CREATE TABLE Former_employees
(name       CHAR(10)
SS_no       CHAR(12)
title       CHAR(8));

INSERT
INTO        Former_employees
            SELECT*
            FROM            Employees
            WHERE           name = 'Gray';

DELETE
FROM        Employees
WHERE       name = 'Gray';
```

8.4
```
DROP TABLE Applicants;
```

8.5
```
SELECT      name,     address,
            SS_no
FROM        Employees
WHERE       title   =   'account-
            ants';
```

8.6
```
CREATE VIEW accountants
AS          SELECT *
            FROM            employees
            WHERE           title = 'accountant';
```

8.7
```
UPDATE      Employees
SET         salary   =   salary   *
            1.05
WHERE       title = 'accountant';
```

8.8
```
UPDATE      Employees
SET         salary   =   salary   *
            1.05;
```

8.9
```
UPDATE    suppliers
SET       city = 'Atlanta'
WHERE     name = 'Alcoe';
```

8.10
```
CREATE VIEW salesmen
AS        SELECT    name, salary
          FROM      Employees
          WHERE     title = 'salesman';
```

9
CHAPTER

Using data control statements

Certain statements provide a database administrator (DBA) with the power to control access to the database, and to institute procedures to preserve the integrity of the data. These considerations take on added significance in a multi-user system where concurrent usage could lead to confusion among users and disruption of the system.

The ORACLE SQL commands that exercise control over database access are GRANT and REVOKE. The basic SQL commands that preserve data integrity are COMMIT, SAVEPOINT, and ROLLBACK.

Access control

Even in single-user systems it might be necessary to control access to the database, and to change access privileges from time to time. The GRANT and REVOKE commands provide a wide range of possibilities for access control.

GRANT

The GRANT command can be used to allow either full access to the database, or limited degrees of access. For example, the type of access granted can be defined in terms of simply looking at database tables; looking at and updating tables; looking only at views; looking at and updating views; or complete access to all tables and views together with the privileges of updating and granting access privileges to other users.

In this context, views combined with the access commands can safeguard specified columns in a table. To do so, set up a view of the table containing only those columns that are not confidential, while omitting the confidential columns from the view. Then grant access to the view, rather than to the table itself. This procedure will be illustrated in the next section.

The syntax of the GRANT command is:

```
GRANT     <specified_access> ON <tablename|viewname>
TO        <grantee_name>, <grantee_id>;
```

where grantee_name is the name to be entered by the user who is being granted the privilege, whenever that user logs onto the system, and grantee_id is the password to be used by the privileged user in logging onto the system.

ORACLE has its own ID system that is separate from the operating system IDs. However, the DBA may grant automatic logins to certain users, tying their ORACLE IDs to operating system IDs. When this is the case, OPS$ is used as a prefix in granting the automatic login, as shown below:

```
GRANT <specified_access> TO OPS$<opsys_id> IDENTIFIED BY
        <password>;
```

Some types of access may carry the privilege of, in turn, granting access to other users. If tables in the database are identified with the name of the creator of the table, then that user (if he or she has been given the appropriate privilege) may grant other users access to his or her tables.

For example, the owner has given Administrative Assistant Barber access to all of the tables with the following command:

```
GRANT ALL PRIVILEGES
TO     Barber
WITH GRANT OPTION;
```

He has now hired a secretary who does the billing under Ms. Barber's direction. Therefore the secretary, Ms. Doe, needs access to the Supplier table and the Customer table. The DBA gave Barber the right to grant access wherever necessary by adding WITH GRANT OPTION to his grant statement to her. Now Ms. Barber, in turn can grant access to specific tables to Ms. Doe.

If Ms. Barber has created other tables or views, which she can do under the terms of her privileges, she has the inherent right to grant anyone else who has access to the database, access to those tables or views that she created.

Ms. Barber can, because of the WITH GRANT OPTION stated in her own privileges, issue the following privileges to Ms. Doe:

```
GRANT ALL PRIVILEGES ON suppliers, customers
TO      Doe;
```

With this command, Ms. Barber gives Ms. Doe the right to update, insert, and delete rows in the Suppliers table and in the Customers table. It also gives Ms. Doe the privilege of dropping both of these tables as well as to create indices on them, to create views on them, and to use all of the data manipulation statements on the views. The GRANT statement does not give Ms. Doe the right to pass on her privileges to other users because the clause WITH GRANT OPTION was not included. However, if Ms. Doe creates a view on either the Suppliers or the Customers tables, she can give other users the right to query that view, and to make changes in it, because she "owns" the views she creates.

Granting access to specified columns only Doe's use of the Suppliers and Customers tables involves using only the Part No. and Price columns, therefore Barber might wish to limit Doe's access to those columns. The command to do this is:

```
GRANT ALL PRIVILEGES(part_no, price)
ON Suppliers, Customers
TO      Doe;
```

This command allows Doe to perform any data manipulation operation—for example SELECT, UPDATE, INSERT, and DELETE—on the Suppliers and Customers tables, but only on the specified columns of those tables.

Granting access to several specified users at once If it is necessary for some personnel, but not all, to use certain tables and/or views, these users can all be named in one GRANT statement. For example, if the secretary (Doe) and the accountants (Walters and Riley) need access to the Suppliers table, then this can be handled with one GRANT statement, as follows:

```
GRANT ALL PRIVILEGES ON Suppliers
TO      Doe, Walters, Riley;
```

The grantee PUBLIC It might be convenient or necessary to make some tables or views available to everyone in the company. Rather than granting access (especially in a large company) to each individual by name, it is much more efficient for the DBA to be able to do this with one command. This is the purpose of the grantee called PUBLIC. Any table or view where PUBLIC is granted access is available to anyone in the organization possessing an ID for entering the database.

At the same time, PUBLIC access might be for reading the table only, not for changing it. If this is the case, then the GRANT statement would be:

```
GRANT SELECT
ON     Suppliers
TO     PUBLIC;
```

If, however, there is a possibility that many persons might need to change the address of a supplier, then it should be possible for anyone to do so. This additional privilege can be granted by allowing update privileges to all, with the following statement:

```
GRANT UPDATE
ON     Suppliers
TO     PUBLIC;
```

If the list of customers is frequently being enlarged by the salespeople, then the opportunity to add to this list can be made available to them, as well as to everyone else, by the statement:

```
GRANT INSERT
ON     Customers
TO     PUBLIC;
```

This command allows anyone in the organization who is authorized to use the database, the opportunity to add rows to the Customers table.

REVOKE

Revoking access is simply the reverse of granting. It is accomplished by using the term REVOKE, naming the type of privilege previously granted, then listing the name and ID of the person whose access is being stopped. If different types of access have been granted to different people, then by selectively revoking, either some or all of these levels can be made unavailable to specified persons. The syntax is:

```
REVOKE   <specified_privileges>
FROM     <username>, <userid>;
```

For example, if at some later time, Ms. Barber leaves the company, the DBA will want to revoke all of her privileges. You can do this by using the command:

```
REVOKE ALL PRIVILEGES
FROM     Barber;
```

This might not leave in place the access(es) she has granted to other members of the firm. Access privileges *cascade* downward, for example the DBA gives privileges to Barber, who gives privileges to Doe, who may give privileges to Jones, etc. But if Barber's privileges are revoked, then any privileges she gave are also revoked, and so on down the line all the way to Jones (and beyond). Therefore, revoking the privileges of one employee might disrupt the entire system as the REVOKE command also cascades by automatically revoking these granted privileges.

Views as security devices

This topic is covered in chapter 11 which is devoted exclusively to views. In general, one of the prime reasons for using views rather than base tables, is to restrict the use of certain parts of the table. Thus, views can be an important part of the security system of the database.

Integrity control

The DCL commands COMMIT, SAVEPOINT, and ROLLBACK are essential to preserving database integrity when you are entering a series of steps that constitute elements of a single transaction.

The ORACLE RDBMS contains a set of LOCK commands to prevent values from changing while a user is looking at, or working with them. These LOCK commands include SHARED LOCK provisions so that several users may access database objects at the same time without long waiting periods.

Control statements also include various AUDIT commands that provide a running record for the DBA as to which users are using which tables or views.

COMMIT

The use of the COMMIT command allows user discretion as to when changes being made actually impinge upon the database. In this context, it is convenient to employ the concept of a transaction as discussed in the next section.

Transactions A *transaction* is a sequence of operations such that each operation in the sequence is necessary to complete a unitary result. In other words, if only part of the sequence were completed and entered into the database, then the database would be (or could be) in a state of imbalance, or error. For example, if parts are sold and these parts are not removed from the inventory list, then the inventory list will show more parts than are actually on hand. Similarly, if, for example, a payment is made to a creditor's account, and the amount of this payment is not deducted from a bank balance, then the bank balance will be in error.

If a transaction requires that changes be made in several columns, or in several tables, it might be that partial recording of that change will cause inconsistencies in the database. For example, entering the fact that an order has been filled might require: (1) deducting the quantity and type of the part from inventory; (2) entering details of the shipment to the customer; (3) entering the amount now due from the customer; and (4) adding the amount due to income receivable by the user. When some, but not all four of these items have been entered, the database will contain incompatible information.

Should a system breakdown occur in the course of such a sequence of entries, it might be time-consuming (or even impossible) to find the inconsistency and restore consistency to the database.

For that reason, SQL provides the user with the option of committing changes to the database only when the transaction is complete. This is done with the command:

```
COMMIT [WORK];
```

A transaction, or part of a transaction that has not yet been committed is visible only to the user entering it. It does not affect the database until the COMMIT statement is executed. Before the execution of the COMMIT statement, it can be rolled back, or eliminated, as discussed in the next section. After a transaction is committed, it cannot be rolled back. If it has to be changed or corrected, that change must be done by means of another SQL statement such as UPDATE or DELETE.

SAVEPOINT

ORACLE SQL provides you with the command SAVEPOINT for long transactions with several parts. This allows you to go back and check and correct parts without executing the entire program. With this command, you can identify a point in a transaction to which you can later rollback with the ROLLBACK TO SAVEPOINT command.

You can use more than one savepoint in the course of entering a long transaction. The default number of savepoints is five, but you can increase this limit by changing the value for the INIT.ORA parameter SAVEPOINTS. The maximum limit is 255 active savepoints.

In an interactive program, you can create and name intermediate steps of a procedure, thus giving you more control over long complex procedures, such as a long series of updates. Thus, if you make an error, you don't have to re-insert every statement.

In application programs, you can use savepoints in a similar way. If you are dealing with several functions, you can create a savepoint before each function begins. Thus, if one function fails, it is easy to return the data to the way it was before the function began and then re-execute it.

You must give each savepoint within a transaction a distinct name. If you use the same savepoint name again, it will erase the earlier savepoint. The form for the SAVEPOINT statement is:

```
SAVEPOINT <savepoint_name>;
```

For example:

```
SAVEPOINT alpha:
```

After you create a savepoint, you can either continue processing, commit your work, rollback the entire transaction, or rollback to the savepoint.

ROLLBACK

If in the course of entering a transaction, an error is made, or if a transaction for some reason cannot (or should not, as for example, during a training session) be completed, the user might want to remove the changes in order to avoid inconsistencies in the database. The command ROLLBACK is supplied for this purpose.

For example, if a new employee was shown how to update, and the training process made partial changes in some tables, then you could use the ROLLBACK command to restore the database to its position before the start of this transaction—to where it was after the last COMMIT statement. The syntax is:

```
ROLLBACK [WORK];
```

This command removes all changes made in the entire transaction that were not followed by a COMMIT statement.

If you have used savepoints at intervals in the transaction, then you can rollback only the part of the transaction that you want to change with the command:

```
ROLLBACK TO SAVEPOINT <savepoint_name>;
```

For example:

```
ROLLBACK TO SAVEPOINT beta:
```

Summary

The data control statements GRANT and REVOKE that control access to the database were illustrated. Transaction processing was explained, as were the basic integrity control commands COMMIT SAVEPOINT and ROLLBACK.

Chapter 9 exercises

The following exercises refer to a table called New Suppliers defined as follows:

```
CREATE TABLE new_suppliers
    (Name          CHAR(20)
    Address        CHAR(30)
    Phone          NUM(10)
    Part_Name      CHAR(12)
    Price          NUM(8)
    Terms          NUM(6)
    Rating         NUM(3));
```

Write SQL statements to:

9.1 Give Martin SELECT privileges over the columns Name, Address, Phone, Part Name and Price.

9.2 Give Smith UPDATE privileges over the entire table.

9.3 Give Fox full privileges over the entire table.

9.4 Give Brown SELECT privileges over the entire table.

9.5 Cancel all of Harro's privileges (assume he had all privileges) except SELECT on the entire table.

9.6 Remove all UPDATE privileges granted to users in exercises 9.1 through 9.5.

9.7 Remove all privileges from Martin.

9.8 Give Fox the right to give the same privileges he now holds to any other employees.

9.9 Give everyone in the organization the privilege of seeing the information in the New Suppliers table.

9.10 Remove the privileges given in exercise 9.9.

Answers to chapter 9 exercises

9.1
```
GRANT SELECT(name, address, phone, part_name, price)
ON New_suppliers
TO Martin;
```

9.2
```
GRANT UPDATE
ON New_suppliers
TO Smith;
```

9.3
```
GRANT ALL PRIVILEGES
ON New_suppliers
TO Fox;
```

9.4
```
GRANT SELECT
ON New_suppliers
TO Brown;
```

9.5
```
REVOKE UPDATE, INSERT, DELETE
ON New_suppliers
FROM Harro;
```

9.6
```
REVOKE UPDATE
ON New_suppliers
FROM Smith, Fox;
```

9.7
```
REVOKE SELECT
ON New_suppliers
FROM Martin;
```

9.8
```
GRANT SELECT, INSERT, DELETE
ON New_suppliers
TO Fox
WITH GRANT OPTION;
```

9.9
```
GRANT SELECT
ON New_suppliers
TO PUBLIC;
```

9.10
```
REVOKE SELECT
ON New_suppliers
FROM PUBLIC;
```

10
CHAPTER

Joins

The ability to retrieve data from two or more tables by matching values in columns is one of SQL's most powerful characteristics. This is the process of forming a join. For example, if you have one table containing employees' names and Social Security Numbers, and another table containing Social Security Numbers and salaries, you can match those rows having the same Social Security Numbers to obtain a table containing the employees' names and salaries.

You might wonder why the salaries would be in a different table from the names. There are many reasons for separating the data about employees into different tables, for example security. You might want to give some people access to the employees' names, but you might not want those same people to have access to employees' salaries.

Another reason for separating data into different tables is to avoid redundancy. Suppose you have a salary history for each employee. In that case you might have a salary table with many entries for each employee, for example his or her salary in 1980, his or her salary in 1981, etc. If you keep the salary history in the same table with other information about the employee, you will have a row with the same data about the employee for every change in salary. The number of occurrences of the rest of the data will be multiplied by the number of changes in salary. If you add information about the employees' children such as their names, ages, and birth dates, the number of rows will be multiplied again by the number of children. And what about those employees with no children? Suppose, then, that you have to update an employee name because of marriage or divorce. You will have to update many rows and you might miss one.

Thus, for security reasons and/or to keep the database consistent and avoid redundancy, it is a good idea to break your tables up into many smaller tables. The best way to do this is found in the theory of database design and is beyond the scope of this book. (See the Bibliography entries for Hursch 1988, Hursch 1989, and Maier for more information on this subject.)

Thus, in relational databases, the information you want might have to come from several different tables. Combining data from different tables involves "joining" the tables together. The resulting table is called a *join*. Sometimes, you might need to join a table with itself. For example, if you have a database of people of both sexes who want dates, containing a lot of people in one table, you might need to match opposite sexes on certain characteristics. The result would be a *self-join*.

The purpose of joining is to create a table that contains rows of relevantly matched information. Then, the data within the single rows of this new table will give you the combination of information you need.

This chapter will explore and illustrate equijoins, non-equijoins, natural joins, theta joins, outer joins, joining more than two tables, joining a table with itself, joining tables to views, and joining views to views.

ORACLE provides a demonstration database containing tables Emp, Dept, Bonus, and Salgrade. Because these tables are available to you if you have a copy of ORACLE, they will be used here for many of the examples. Sometimes other tables are required to make a specific point so other examples will also be provided. To set up these tables, you must run the executable program DEMOBLD. For information on DEMOBLD, consult your ORACLE *Installation and User's Guide*. You can try using these demonstration tables in SQL*Plus at the SQL prompt.

The ORACLE demonstration tables have the following columns:

Emp:

Column name	**Datatype**
empno	Not null number(4)
ename	char(10)
job	char(9)
mgr	number(4)
hiredate	date
sal	number(7,2)
comm	number(7,2)
deptno	number(2)

Dept:

Column name	**Datatype**
deptno	number(2)
dname	char(14)
loc	char(13)

Bonus:

Column name	**Datatype**
ename	char(10)
job	char(9)
sal	number
comm	number

Salgrade:

Column name	**Datatype**
grade	number
losal	number
hisal	number

In our version of ORACLE the tables are initialized to have the following rows:

Emp:

empno	**ename**	**job**	**mgr**	**hiredate**	**sal**	**comm**	**deptno**
7369	SMITH	CLERK	7902	17-DEC-80	800		20
7499	ALLEN	SALESMAN	7698	20-FEB-81	1,600	300	30
7521	WARD	SALESMAN	7698	22-FEB-81	1,250	500	30
7566	JONES	MANAGER	7839	02-APR-81	2,975		20
7654	MARTIN	SALESMAN	7698	28-SEP-81	1,250	1400	30
7698	BLAKE	MANAGER	7839	01-MAY-81	2,850		30
7782	CLARK	MANAGER	7839	09-JUN-81	2,450		10
7788	SCOTT	ANALYST	7566	09-DEC-82	3,000		20
7839	KING	PRESIDENT		17-NOV-81	5,000		10
7844	TURNER	SALESMAN	7698	08-SEP-81	1,500	0	30
7876	ADAMS	CLERK	7788	12-JAN-83	1,100		20
7900	JAMES	CLERK	7698	03-DEC-81	950		30
7902	FORD	ANALYST	7566	03-DEC-81	3,000		20
7934	MILLER	CLERK	7782	23-JAN-82	1,300		10

Dept:

deptno	**dname**	**loc**
10	ACCOUNTING	NEW YORK
20	RESEARCH	DALLAS
30	SALES	CHICAGO
40	OPERATIONS	BOSTON

Bonus has nothing in it. However the SQL statement:

```
INSERT INTO BONUS SELECT ENAME,JOB,SAL,COMM FROM EMP
WHERE JOB = 'SALESMAN',
```

initializes it to the following table:

Bonus:

ENAME	JOB	SAL	COMM
ALLEN	SALESMAN	1600	300
WARD	SALESMAN	1250	500
MARTIN	SALESMAN	1250	1400
TURNER	SALESMAN	1500	0

SALGRADE:

GRADE	LOSAL	HISAL
1	700	1200
2	1201	1400
3	1401	2000
4	2001	3000
5	3001	9999

Sometimes additional sample tables are provided with your version of ORACLE. The version of ORACLE that we have provides the tables Customer, Item, Ord, Price, Product, and Seq. To see what tables you have, try the query:

```
SELECT * FROM CATALOG;
```

To find the column names and types in these tables, you can use Oracle's DESCRIBE command. For example:

```
DESCRIBE EMP
```

will produce a display of the columns and column types for the table Emp.

If this display goes by too fast for you to read it, you can print it out by pressing Ctrl-Prtsc before issuing the command. When you want to stop printing, press Ctrl-Prtsc again. If you don't have an attached printer you can *spool* everything to a file by issuing the SQL*Plus command:

```
SPOOL <filename>
```

When you have recorded what you want, type SPOOL OFF and press Return. To read the resulting file at your leisure, type the following at the SQL prompt:

```
$type <filename> | more
```

and press Return. The $ sign allows you to execute a DOS command. The | more pipes the output from the type command to the DOS more command. The more command lets you observe one page at a time.

Equijoins

The general format for an equijoin between two tables is:

```
SELECT   <alias1.columns>, <alias2.columns>
FROM     <table1> <alias1>, <table2> <alias2>
WHERE    <conditions>;
```

where the comparison operator in the <conditions> is a set of equal signs between columns ANDed together, and <alias1.columns> is a list of one or more columns from table1.

The columns compared must be of the same datatype and width. For example, if you have a table containing raingages and their locations at given latitudes and longitudes and another table containing rain observations at given latitudes and longitudes, you might want to join the two tables to find which gages registered the amounts. You can do this with the following join:

```
SELECT   R.raingage_id,O.amount_of_rain
FROM     raingages R,observations O
WHERE    R.latitude = O.latitude
AND      R.longitude = O.longitude;
```

Note that, technically, this query does not yield just a join, but rather a join followed by a projection on the columns raingage_id and amount_of_rain. This is always the case when all of the columns from both tables do not appear in the SELECT clause. See chapter 14 for an explanation.

Usually you will want to obtain an equijoin where two tables have one or more common columns, and the <set of conditions> in the WHERE clause is that the values in the common columns are equal. The common columns are called the *join columns*.

It is necessary to use the table name or alias identification with each occurrence of the join column to make it clear that the occurrences come from different tables. (Aliases are discussed in chapter 6.)

For example:

```
SELECT E.ENAME,D.LOC FROM EMP E,DEPT D
WHERE E.DEPTNO = D.DEPTNO;
```

yields the following table:

ENAME	LOC
CLARK	NEW YORK
MILLER	NEW YORK
KING	NEW YORK
SMITH	DALLAS
SCOTT	DALLAS
JONES	DALLAS

ENAME	LOC
ADAMS	DALLAS
FORD	DALLAS
ALLEN	CHICAGO
BLAKE	CHICAGO
TURNER	CHICAGO
JAMES	CHICAGO
MARTIN	CHICAGO
WARD	CHICAGO

The E and D are aliases for the tables Emp and Dept respectively, and serve the purpose of identifying the table containing the column selected. Aliases are sometimes called *correlation variables* or *range variables.* They have the advantage of providing a short abbreviation for the table name. In general, it is a good idea to use aliases if you list more than one table in the FROM clause.

The previous query could also be written:

```
SELECT   emp.ename, dept.loc
FROM     emp, dept
WHERE    emp.deptno = dept.deptno;
```

The Cartesian product

If the set of conditions in the equijoin shown in first section of this chapter is empty—if there aren't any conditions, which is technically a special case—then the result is the *Cartesian product*. In other words, by juxtaposing each row of one table with each row of another table (without eliminating any rows of either table) the result is the Cartesian product of the two tables. In the case of the Cartesian product there is no WHERE clause. The syntax for doing this is:

```
SELECT   *
FROM     <table1>, <table2>;
```

For example, consider the following Table 1 containing columns A and B, and Table 2 containing columns C and D:

Table 1		**Table 2**	
A	**B**	**C**	**D**
4	3	6	5
1	9	2	7

The Cartesian product of Tables 1 and 2 is Table 3 containing columns A, B, C, and D:

Table 3

A	B	C	D
4	3	6	5
4	3	2	7
1	9	6	5
1	9	2	7

The number of rows in the Cartesian product of two tables is the product of the number of rows in each of the tables because each of the rows in the first table is paired with each of the rows in the second table. For example, the Cartesian product of Dept with Salgrade contains 20 rows because there are four rows in Dept and five rows in Salgrade.

To test this for yourself, try this query:

```
SELECT * FROM DEPT,SALGRADE;
```

The order of the rows in the Cartesian product is not relevant. If you want to order the rows in a specific way, you must add an ORDER BY clause to the SELECT statement. If you do not add an ORDER BY clause, the order of the rows in the result table will depend on the way the system you are working with has been programmed; and, thus, the ordering will vary from database system to database system.

The number of rows in a Cartesian product is the multiplicative product of the number of rows in the tables. In general, the Cartesian product is hardly ever useful. In order to obtain a useful result, you need to match rows in some way using a WHERE clause. The rows obtained when you match rows, using a WHERE clause, will always be a subset of the Cartesian product.

The natural join

Technically, the *equijoin* between two or more tables is defined as being the table constructed from all of the columns in each of the tables by matching on common columns. For details see chapter 14.

The *natural join*, which is usually referred to simply as a *join*, is obtained by taking an equijoin on the common columns of two tables and then removing the duplicated columns.

For example, Dept and Emp have the column Deptno in common. In order to obtain the natural join of Dept and Emp you would use the following query:

```
SELECT
EMPNO,ENAME,JOB,MGR,HIREDATE,SALARY,COMM,
E.DEPTNO,DNAME,LOC FROM EMP E,DEPT D WHERE
E.DEPTNO = D.DEPTNO;
```

Notice that it is necessary to name all the columns in order to avoid repeating the column Deptno. The following query:

```
SELECT * FROM EMP E,DEPT D WHERE E.DEPTNO
= D.DEPTNO;
```

would repeat the column Deptno and is an equijoin but not a natural join because the column Deptno is repeated.

Join on specified columns only

If you do not want to display all of the columns that appear in the natural join, then you can form a join of specified columns by listing the columns you want after the SELECT command:

```
SELECT    <table1.columns>, <table2.columns>
FROM      <table1>, <table2>
WHERE     <join_column1> = <join_column2>;
```

This means that the retrieval will consist of the columns you want displayed from Table 1 and Table 2 wherever the row value in the join column in Table 1 is the same as the row value in the join column in Table 2.

As an example, suppose you wanted to assign customers to salesmen who live in the same district as the customer. Given that you have a Salesmen table listing only salesmen and their districts, and a Customer table showing only customers and their districts, you would then join the Salesmen table to the Customer table wherever the salesman's district matched the customer's district, as follows:

```
SELECT      salesmen, customers
FROM        salesmen, customers
WHERE       salesmen.district = customer.district
GROUP BY    district;
```

Note that the column names in the WHERE clause are qualified by preceding them with the table name. This is because these columns have the same name in each of the tables, and the column name alone would be ambiguous. (However, join columns do not have to have the same name.)

The equijoin will retrieve the columns requested, and among these will be two identical columns, for example join_column1 and join_column2 both contain the District column. The results will look like this:

Salesman name	District	Customer name	District
Fox	Southpark	Minton	Southpark
Fox	Southpark	Winters	Southpark
Fox	Southpark	Summers	Southpark
Smith	Northpark	Barnes	Northpark

Salesman name	District	Customer name	District
Smith	Northpark	Gaylord	Northpark
Harro	Westerly	Carter	Westerly
Baker	Eastern	Sutton	Eastern
Baker	Eastern	Wiley	Eastern

To obtain this join without the duplicate District column, select all columns from either table. Then select the necessary column in the other table and leave out the column that would be a duplicate. The following query selects all columns from the Salesmen table and only the name column from the Customer table:

```
SELECT      salesmen.*, customers.name
FROM        salesmen, customers
WHERE       salesmen.district = customer.district
GROUP BY    district;
```

The result will show only one District column.

Salesman name	District	Customer name
Fox	Southpark	Minton
Fox	Southpark	Winters
Fox	Southpark	Summers
Smith	Northpark	Barnes
Smith	Northpark	Gaylord
Harro	Westerly	Carter
Baker	Eastern	Sutton
Baker	Eastern	Wiley

In practice, you will only select columns that contain the information you need. Frequently you will leave out the join columns and several other columns to make the result easier to read and understand. For example in:

```
SELECT   R.raingage_id,O.amount_of_rain
FROM     raingages R,observations O
WHERE    R.latitude = O.latitude
AND      R.longitude = O.longitude;
```

the join columns never appear in the result table. For example, if raingages has the two rows:

raingage_id	latitude	longitude
GUCO2	91	34
TXDT4	85	41

and observations has the two rows:

amount_of_rain	latitude	longitude
2.5	91	34
3.6	85	41

then the result table will have the following two rows:

raingage_id	amount_of_rain
GUCO2	2.5
TXDT4	3.6

To try this idea with the example tables provided with ORACLE, try the following query:

```
SELECT EMP.ENAME,DEPT.* FROM EMP,DEPT
WHERE EMP.DEPTNO = DEPT.DEPTNO;
```

Non-equijoins

A *non-equijoin* exists when two tables are joined and the join column in one table is not equal to the corresponding join column in the other table. The general syntax for a non-equijoin is:

```
SELECT    <table1.columns>, <table2.columns>
FROM      <table1>, <table2>
WHERE     <join_column1>
          (<any comparison operator except =) join_column2>);
```

where the comparison operator may be:

greater than	>
greater than or equal	> =
less than	<
less than or equal	< =
not equal to	! = ,^ = , < >

For example, instead of assigning salesmen to customers in the same districts as those in which the salesmen live, you could do it the other way: assign salesmen to customers who do not live in their home districts. To do this, enter:

```
SELECT    salesmen.*, customers.*
FROM      salesmen, customers
WHERE     NOT salesmen.districts = customers.districts;
```

Or, the WHERE clause could be entered as:

```
WHERE   salesmen.districts < > customers.districts;
```

The result would match salesmen with customers unpredictably except that there would be no rows where the salesman district was the same as the customer's district. (Note that the NOT must come before the search condition as shown. The expression:

```
WHERE salesmen.districts NOT = customer.district
```

is not a legal form of the predicate.)

BETWEEN is also an operator that can result in a non-equijoin. For example, try the following query:

```
SELECT E.ENAME,S.GRADE FROM EMP E,SALGRADE S
WHERE E.SAL BETWEEN S.LOSAL AND S.HISAL;
```

Equijoins and non-equijoins together form a class of joins called *theta joins*.

Additional conditions in join queries

The WHERE clause in a join query may be used to specify any number of conditions. To do so, use an AND to specify the additional condition(s). If the salesmen discussed in the preceding sections were actually listed in a table containing all employees, then you would want to qualify the query so that the secretary, the accountant, and the programmers would not be linked with customers. To do this, put another condition in the join query like this:

```
SELECT   employee.name, customer.name
FROM     employees, customers
WHERE    employee.district = customer.district
AND      employee.title = 'salesman';
```

This query will join salesmen with customers according to matching districts, without matching any non-sales personnel with customers.

Here is a query that uses the ORACLE example tables and adds an additional condition:

```
SELECT E.ENAME,S.GRADE FROM EMP E,SALGRADE S
WHERE E.SAL BETWEEN S.LOSAL AND S.HISAL
AND E.JOB = 'SALESMAN';
```

Any number of conditions may be added to the WHERE clause by the use of the AND operator.

Joining more than two tables

Any number of tables can be joined. To do this, put the name of the tables to be joined in the FROM clause and use the AND operator to add any conditions necessary. For example:

```
SELECT    <aliases.column__names>
FROM      <table1 alias1,table2, ... ,tablen aliasn>
WHERE     <condition1>
AND       <condition2>
...
AND       <conditionM>;
```

For example, the following query joins the Emp, Dept, and Salgrade tables:

```
SELECT * FROM EMP E,DEPT D,SALGRADE S
WHERE E.DEPTNO = D.DEPTNO
AND E.SAL BETWEEN S.LOSAL AND S.HISAL;
```

Joining tables to views

You can join one or more tables with one or more views the same way you join a table to a table. For example, if you want to join an entire view to only certain columns of a table, use the following:

```
SELECT    <viewname.*>, <tablename.column1>,
          <tablename.column2>, <tablename.columnN>
FROM      <viewname>, <tablename>
WHERE     <join condition>;
```

To try this with the ORACLE example tables, first create a view called Empsub as follows:

```
CREATE VIEW EMPSUB AS
SELECT ENAME,JOB,DEPTNO FROM EMP;
```

Then try the query:

```
SELECT EMPSUB.*,DEPT.DNAME FROM EMPSUB,DEPT
WHERE EMPSUB.DEPTNO = DEPT.DEPTNO;
```

Or, use aliases:

```
SELECT E.*,D.DNAME FROM EMPSUB E DEPT D
WHERE E.DEPTNO = D.DEPTNO;
```

This illustrates the fact that for query purposes a view is just like a table.

Creating a view from a join

You can create a view and form a join from two or more tables simultaneously by adding the SELECT statement as a subquery and specifying the join commands in the CREATE VIEW statement as follows:

```
CREATE VIEW <viewname> <column__name, column__name ...>
```

```
AS <subquery>
```

where <subquery> is any SELECT statement.

Let's say you wanted to join just the salesmen's names and districts with the customer names and districts in the example shown in the earlier section of this chapter entitled "Additional conditions in join queries." In that example, salesmen are listed in the Employees table. Therefore, it would be better to create a view called Assignments instead of using both tables. To do so, enter:

```
CREATE VIEW assignments
AS   SELECT     employee.name, employee.district, customer.name,
                customer.district
     FROM       employees, customers
     WHERE      employee.district = customer.district
     AND        title = 'salesman'
     ORDER BY   district;
```

This would yield the view called Assignments, showing only the salesmen's names and districts, linked with the customer's names by district.

Using the ORACLE example tables you can create the view Empgrade as follows:

```
CREATE VIEW EMPGRADE AS
SELECT E.ENAME,S.GRADE FROM EMP E. SALGRADE S
WHERE E.SAL BETWEEN S.LOSAL AND S.HISAL;
```

It is important to realize that a view is not a table, but rather a prescription for a result table that is entirely dependent on the base tables named in the FROM clause of the SELECT statement. For example, if you select everything from Empgrade, add a new employee to Emp, and then select everything again, the second select will reflect the change in Emp. You should try this by first entering:

```
SELECT * FROM EMPGRADE;
```

then enter:

```
INSERT INTO EMP (EMPNO,ENAME,SAL)
VALUES (555,'ALGER',3500);
```

then try:

```
SELECT * FROM EMPGRADE;
```

again.

Notice that after the second select the row, ALGER 5, has been added to Empgrade reflecting the insertion into Emp.

To get rid of the extra row in Emp, use the ROLLBACK statement.

To see your view definitions, try the following query:

```
SELECT * FROM VIEWS;
```

Joining views to views

Views can be joined to views in the same way that tables are joined to tables. The names of the views being joined should appear after the FROM clause just as tables being joined are named in the FROM clause. To test this, try the following query:

```
SELECT * FROM EMPSUB ES,EMPGRADE EG
WHERE ES.ENAME = EG.ENAME;
```

Joining a table with itself

There might be times when you want to join rows in the same table. This is a good time to use aliases. For example, you might want a list of pairs of salesmen who are in the same city. To do this, you must list the table twice in the FROM clause and then distinguish the two listings by giving each an alias. For the query: List all pairs of salesmen who are in the same city, enter:

```
SELECT    First.name, Second.name
FROM      Salesmen First, Salesmen Second
WHERE     First.City = Second.City
AND       First.SS# < Second.SS#;
```

where SS# is the salesman's Social Security Number. The FROM clause assigns the alias First to the Salesmen table, and the alias Second to the same Salesmen table. The specification after the AND, where the first SS# must be greater than the second, prevents the result from showing a salesman paired with himself (Jones, Jones), and prevents it from showing the same pairing twice, as for example (Jones, Smith) and (Smith, Jones).

For some queries, there are other ways to combine a table with itself, but use of aliases often makes the meaning clearer.

To try the above with the ORACLE example tables, try:

```
SELECT E1.ENAME,E2.ENAME FROM EMP E1,EMP E2
WHERE E1.SAL = E2.SAL
AND E1.ENAME != E2.ENAME;
```

Outer joins

In some situations it might be useful to retrieve rows that meet one of the join conditions, but not both. Such cases are called *outer joins*.

Outer joins are important because they might retrieve data that can otherwise be lost if the join condition alone is used for retrieval. For example, a join column might contain rows that would fit the join condition except that they have NULL values in the second join column or the values are not matched in the second table. It might be that if those NULL values were filled in with non-NULL values, the join condition would be completely satisfied. With the join retrieval, these rows would not be picked up. An outer join retrieval would return these rows; they can then be examined to determine whether or not supplying the missing values would satisfy the join condition.

It might be helpful in conceptualizing outer joins to realize that joins are analogous to the intersection of sets (the join includes all rows that are members of both sets) and outer joins are analogous to the (exclusive) UNION of sets. In other words, the outer join includes rows that are members of one, but not both, of the specified sets.

ORACLE supplies a special symbol for the outer join: the plus sign (+). This symbol actually causes the outer join rows to be added to the usual rows by adding an extra empty row to the column it follows in the WHERE clause. To see this try the query:

```
SELECT E.DEPTNO,D.DEPTNO FROM EMP E,DEPT D
WHERE E.DEPTNO (+) = D.DEPTNO;
```

The result table has an extra row with 40 in the second column. If you put the + after D.DEPTNO, you won't get any unmatched rows because all of the Deptnos in the Emp table are matched by Deptnos in the Dept table.

Outer joins are not supported directly by the SQL language, although E.F. Codd referred to them, and set forth the requirements for an *outer join syntax*. (See the Bibliography for entries on Codd's 1979 ACM paper and his 1990 book, D.D. Chamberlin's 1980 paper, and C.J. Date's *Relational Database: Selected Writings* to find more information on this topic.)

The query used by ORACLE to retrieve the outer join is set up this way:

```
SELECT    <table1.columns>, <table2.columns>
FROM      <table1, table2>
WHERE     <join_column1> = <join_column2>(+);
```

The outer join symbol (+) tells SQL*Plus to treat Table 2 as though it contained an extra row with a NULL value in every column; the interface then joins this NULL row of Table 2 to any row of Table 1 that cannot be joined to an existing row of Table 2. In this way, ORACLE picks up the outer join by combining SQL commands with a special outer join command built into the interface.

The need to retrieve an outer join can be illustrated in the previous matching of salesmen's districts with customers' districts. If there happens to be a customer in a district where no salesman lives there would be no match with this customer. Therefore, there would be no salesman servicing that customer because no row in the join contained that customer.

Conversely, if there were a salesman who lived in a district where there were no customers, this salesman would not be matched with any customer because no row in the join contained that salesman.

Summary

Joins, an especially useful feature of SQL, were explained and illustrated. The many different types of joins involving both tables and views were shown along with explanations of their uses. These included equijoins, non-equijoins, joining more than two tables, joining tables to views, creating a view from a join, joining views to views, joining a table with itself, and outer joins.

Chapter 10 exercises

Use the following tables to complete the exercises below:

Candidates

Name	**District**	**Office**
Smith	7	Council
Breag	3	Council
Jones	3	Mayor
Sherman	6	Council
Olson	6	Coroner
Wilson	4	Council
Black	1	Sheriff
Fortin	2	D.A.
Leery	2	Council

Volunteers

Name	**District**
Deeds	1
Burk	1
Lyman	2
Merrik	2
Martinez	2
Volnik	3
Stacio	4
Rudd	11

Write SQL statements for exercises 10.1 through 10.3:

10.1 For the Cartesian product of Candidates and Volunteers.
10.2 For the natural join of Candidates and Volunteers.
10.3 List the Candidates with the Volunteers who are in the same District.

10.4 Consider the Relay Runner database table:

Runner	**Lap**	**Team**
Jones	1	Golden Angels
Richards	2	Golden Angels
Ignatz	3	Golden Angels
Camp	4	Golden Angels
Williams	1	East
Agronsky	2	East
Stevens	3	East
Smith	4	East

Form a self-join of this table that will give the name of each runner in the same row with the name of the runner to whom he hands the baton.

10.5 Let the Coaches table in the same database be:

Runner	**Coach**
Jones	Wesson
Richards	Caps
Ignatz	Wesson
Camp	Caps
Williams	East
Agronsky	Johanson
Stevens	Johanson
Smith	Mickey

Find the coach for each team.

10.6 Find those coaches whose names are the same as their team.

10.7 Let the Owners table be:

Owner	**Team**
Millions	Golden Angels
Scrooge	East

Find the runners and the owners they work for.

10.8 Find the runners, coaches, and owners that are with the same team.

10.9 Let the Team City table be:

Team	**City**
Golden Angels	Dallas
East	New York

Find the Owners and the City where their team is located.

10.10 Find the runners, coaches, and owners that are with the same team, and the city where they are located.

Answers to chapter 10 exercises

10.1

```
SELECT  candidates.*, volunteers.*
FROM    candidates, volunteers;
```

10.2

```
SELECT  candidates.*, volunteers.name
FROM    candidates, volunteers
WHERE   candidates.district = volunteers.district;
```

10.3

```
SELECT  candidates.*, volunteers.*
FROM    candidates, volunteers
WHERE   candidates.district = volunteers.district;
```

10.4

```
SELECT  First.*, Second.*
FROM    relay_runners
WHERE   First.lap = Second.lap
AND     First.Team = Second.Team;
```

10.5

```
SELECT  Team, Coach
FROM    Relay_runners,Coaches
WHERE   Relay_runners.runner = Coaches.runner;
```

10.6

```
SELECT  Team,Coach
FROM    Relay_runners,Coaches
WHERE   Relay_runners.runner = Coaches.runner
AND     Team = Coach;
```

10.7

```
SELECT  Runner,Owner
FROM    Relay_runners,Owners
WHERE   Relay_runners.Team = Owners.Team;
```

10.8

```
SELECT  runner,Coach,Owner
FROM    Relay_runners,Coaches,Owners
WHERE   Relay_runners.Team = Owners.Team
AND     Relay_runners.runner = Coaches.runner;
```

10.9

```
SELECT  Owner,City
FROM    Owners,Team_city
WHERE   Owners.Team = Team_city.Team;
```

10.10

```
SELECT  Runner,Coach,Owner,City
FROM    Relay_runners,Coaches,Owners,Team_city
WHERE   Relay_runners.Team = Owners.Team
AND     Relay_runners.runner = Coaches.runner
AND     Owners.Team = Team_city.Team;
```

11
CHAPTER

Working with views, indices, and queries

While views have already been encountered earlier in this text, the convenience and security they offer make it worthwhile to consider them in greater detail. Therefore, the early part of this chapter illustrates views in detail.

Queries and indices are discussed further in this chapter because SQL commands specify only what information is wanted, not how to get it out of the database. The ORACLE RDBMS includes a facility for optimizing the access paths to the data being sought. However, the proper database design, based on an understanding of relational theory can contribute to high performance. Also, the end user who becomes thoroughly familiar with ORACLE SQL can enhance the optimization process in two ways by: (1) creating sufficient and appropriate indices; and (2) constructing queries to take advantage of the system.

These two optimization processes are somewhat complementary because an understanding of the purpose and function of indices will lead to the optimal construction of queries.

This chapter will discuss indices in detail, and will also cover the performance advantages inherent in the wording of certain SQL statements.

Views

There are three main purposes for working with views:

1. As a database grows large, it is usually much more convenient to work with a view consisting of selected columns from a table rather than the whole table. A simple query to a view that contains only those columns you intend to work with in a given session can be far easier to construct than a query selecting a few specific columns out of a large table.
2. Tables might contain more information than should prudently be displayed to all employees who might use the database, such as salaries or specifications for new products. If this is the case with a given table, then use of the table itself might be restricted to a few specified employees, while the non-confidential columns are set up as a view and made available to all who work with the database.
3. In large, multi-user systems, views can provide the means for different users to see the same data in different ways, and depending on the capacity of the system, possibly at the same time.

Therefore, working with views can be more convenient than working with a large table. Views can also provide the necessary security for confidential information in the database.

At the same time, views have some disadvantages:

1. Views are not stored in the database. Only the view definition is stored in the catalog; the actual view is recomputed each time it is displayed. Therefore, views might require more processing time than tables.
2. Special techniques must be used when updating, inserting or deleting views based on more than one table. These problems will be discussed as they arise in the sections that follow.

If a view contains a GROUP BY clause or a HAVING clause that is not contained in a subquery, then this is called a *grouped view*.

This chapter will also discuss joining views, using expressions and functions in views, updating views, and using views as part of the data security system.

Creating a view

The syntax for creating a view is:

```
CREATE VIEW <viewname> [(<view target list>)]
AS SELECT <column1_name, column2_name
... columnN _name>
        FROM      <tablename>
        WHERE     <condition>
WITH CHECK OPTION;
```

The view target list, shown in brackets after the viewname, does not have to be specified. If it is specified, it must contain the same number of columns, in the same order, as the target list after the SELECT command.

If the view target list is not specified, then no two columns listed after the SELECT command can have the same name, and there can be no unnamed columns in the table named in the FROM clause.

If the view is updatable (see upcoming section regarding view updating) then WITH CHECK OPTION can be specified. This option will check that the values inserted as updates fit the WHERE condition. If the view is not updatable, then the view is considered to be a read-only table.

As an example of the need for creating a view: assume that the original company set up in chapter 7 has grown so that there are now 12 employees: six salesmen, three clerks, the owner, the secretary, and an accountant. You need to separate out the salesmen from the other employees. To do so, set up a view called Salesmen, as follows:

```
CREATE VIEW Salesmen
AS      SELECT    name, SS_no, salary, commission
        FROM      Employees
        WHERE     job title = 'salesman'
WITH CHECK OPTION;
```

This will create a view named Salesmen, listing the values shown in the four columns listed after the SELECT statement, for only those personnel whose title is salesman. It will look exactly like a base table.

Because the other employees do not receive commissions, using the view will simplify queries when it is necessary to perform operations relating to the commissions received by the salesmen.

At the same time, you can query the view just as you would query any table. If you want to display the contents of the view called Salesmen, you can do it just as you would display all columns of a table:

```
SELECT    *
FROM      Salesmen;
```

This will display the following view called Salesmen, which was created from the base table Employees:

Employee Name	Salesmen SS_no	Salary	Commission
Martin	001 666 6666	900	975
Jones	000 555 5555	1200	900
Smith	000 123 1234	1500	800
Harro	003 321 4331	1350	950
Fox	008 222 2424	950	600
Brown	005 333 4444	850	550

You can use a WHERE clause in querying the view just as you would if it were a base table. For example, if you wanted to display only those salesmen whose salary is higher than a specified figure, you can do it as follows:

```
SELECT    name, salary
FROM      Salesmen
WHERE     salary > 1000;
```

This will produce the following view of the view Salesmen:

Salesmen Employee Name	Salary
Jones	1200
Smith	1500
Harro	1350

At the same time, because a view itself is not stored, it will be affected by any changes made in the base table from which it is derived. When the table is updated, to show that a salesman received a raise, the next time you query the view, you will find that the view exhibits this updated salary figure for that salesman. If the salesman leaves the company, and his name is deleted from the Employees table, then it also will be deleted from the view Salesmen. If a new salesman is added (inserted) to the Employees table, he will be added to the view Salesmen.

Conversely, if you make changes in a view, some, but not all such changes will occur back in the base table from which the view was derived. This is an important fact to keep in mind when working with views. Changes in views that do not change existing data in the base table are discussed as they occur in the following sections.

Views on multiple tables

You may combine columns from several different tables in any one view. For example, salesmen who live in the same city with a supplier sell the products of that supplier, and it would be convenient to have a view listing these. To do this, join the Name column from the Employees table with the appropriate Name column from the Suppliers table wherever a Salesman is in the same city with the supplier. This is accomplished as follows:

```
CREATE VIEW Clients
AS      SELECT    employee.name, supplier_name
        FROM      Employees, Suppliers
        WHERE     title = 'salesman'
        AND       employee.city = supplier.city;
```

Joining a view to another view or to a table

Views may be joined to each other and/or to a table. The syntax for doing this is shown in chapter 10. Keep in mind, however, that a view containing a GROUP BY clause cannot be joined to another view or to a table.

Expressions and functions in views

You may use expressions and functions in a view, but when you do, you must specify names for all the columns in the row. For example, assume you need to convert each employee's monthly salary to an annual salary. You can have the view perform the computation with the following:

```
CREATE VIEW Annual_Salary (employee_name, SS_no, address, title,
                           salary)
AS      SELECT    employee_name, SS_no, address, title, salary * 12
        FROM      Employees;
```

This computed column salary * 12 will not appear back in the base table. It will only be available through the view.

Note that there is no ALTER VIEW statement. The ALTER TABLE statement that adds a column to a table does not add a column to views that are already defined, although views created after the column is added to the table will show the additional column.

Aggregate functions in views

You can use the aggregate functions, COUNT, COUNT(*), SUM, AVG, MAX, MIN, in views. (Aggregate functions are defined and discussed in chapter 6.) For example, to obtain the total amount paid to salesmen, their salary must be added to commission. This can be done by using the Salesmen view created in the "Creating a View" section earlier in this chapter, as follows:

```
SELECT SUM(salary + commission)
FROM     Salesmen;
```

The result will be a one-column, one-row table showing the total salary plus commission paid to all salesmen.

In the same way, you could use any of the other aggregate functions in the view Salesman, just as though the view were a base table. However, these calculated columns will not appear back in the base table Employees from which the view Salesman was drawn.

Updating rows in views

If a view is derived from only one table, then instead of updating the base table, you can update the view in the same way you would update the table. For example, the view Salesmen comes directly out of the Employees table, therefore you can update it as follows:

```
UPDATE    Salesmen
SET       commission = 0.25*salary;
```

This UPDATE statement will set the commission of all salesmen at 25 percent of their salaries.

If, however, a view is the result of a join of two or more tables (discussed in chapter 10) then updating will require a special process in the same way as inserting and deleting.

In general, you may update a view the same way you update a table if it:

- is derived from only one base table.
- does not contain a GROUP BY clause, or a DISTINCT clause.
- does not contain any of the group functions AVERAGE, COUNT(*), COUNT, SUM, MAX or MIN.
- does not contain a field derived from an arithmetic expression or a constant.

Inserting rows into views

You may insert rows into views in the same way that you insert rows into tables if the view is derived from only one table and the view contains all of the NOT NULL columns of the base table.

If the view is the result of a join of two or more tables, then the same cautions apply that were discussed in the previous section regarding updating. In general, you can insert rows into views just as you would insert them into tables if the view:

- refers to only one table.
- does not contain a GROUP BY clause, a DISTINCT clause or a group function.
- contains no columns defined by the group functions AVERAGE, COUNT(*), COUNT, MAX, MIN or SUM.

- includes all of the NOT NULL columns of the base table.
- does not contain a field that is derived from an arithmetic expression or a constant.

Deleting rows from views

The same cautions apply to deleting data from views that were stated with regard to updating and inserting in views except that, unlike updating and inserting, you can delete from a view even though one or more fields are derived from an arithmetic expression or a constant.

In general, you may delete rows from views the same way that you delete from tables if the view:

- is derived from only one table.
- does not contain a GROUP BY clause or a DISTINCT clause.
- does not contain any of the group functions AVERAGE, COUNT, COUNT(*), MAX, MIN or SUM.

Using views to restrict table access

Views can be used to divide up the database into column or row segments of tables. Then, by using the DCL GRANT and REVOKE statements, you can hide confidential information from all but authorized users. For example, if a new user were to be allowed to work with employees names, titles, and Social Security Numbers but not their salaries, the following view could be created:

```
CREATE VIEW Employees_Limited
AS     SELECT    employee_name, SS_no, title
       FROM      Employees;
```

The new user could then be granted access to this view rather than to the complete Employees table where all personnel data are stored, with the following command:

```
GRANT     SELECT, UPDATE(Title)
ON        Employees_Limited
TO        <new_user>, <new_userid>;
```

Or, if the new user's privileges are to be more extensive, the following command can be used:

```
GRANT     ALL PRIVILEGES
ON        Employees_Limited
TO        <new_user>, <new_userid>;
```

In this way, confidential information can be hidden in the table while non-confidential information can be available in the same table to users who need to work with it.

Using indices to optimize performance

Indices have two main purposes:

1. *To improve performance by reducing disk I/O.* Indices in a database perform a function similar to that of indices in a book: they speed up the retrieval of information. This is especially true for information in joined tables.
2. *To ensure uniqueness.* You can create a unique index on a column. Then, if an attempt is made to insert a row that will duplicate a value already in that column, the insertion will be rejected. Therefore, a UNIQUE INDEX command acts as a check on the uniqueness of the column.

Indices and keys

Keys are a part of relational databases but currently they are rarely implemented except through indices. A *candidate key* is a designated column, or group of columns, that uniquely defines a row in a given table. One of the candidate keys can be designated as the *primary key*. A *foreign key* is a designated column in a given table that uniquely defines a row in some other table, such as a candidate key in the other table.

Creating an index on each key will definitely improve query performance. Update performance will not necessarily be improved, and might even be reduced by many indices because the index has to be recomputed after each update. However, there is another reason for maintaining a unique index on all candidate keys: A properly designed database scheme usually has the property that integrity of the database requires that all candidate keys always determine a unique row. The only way to guarantee this is to define a unique index on every candidate key. For more information on maintaining integrity constraints by means of candidate keys, refer to the Bibliography for an entry on D. Maier's treatment of complete database schemes (in his chapter 7).

Unique indices

If you own a table, which means you have created it, or if you have been granted access to a table, you can create an index on it. The syntax for creating a unique index is:

```
CREATE UNIQUE INDEX <index_name>
ON   <table_name>
     <column_name(s)>;
```

where the <column_name(s)> are those columns you want indexed.

You can index as many columns of a table as you wish, but how many columns you index will depend on the purpose of the table: If the table is to be updated frequently, then more indices mean more overhead. If, on the other hand, it is a read-only table or is seldom updated, then it would be advisable to have more indices.

Indices on multiple columns

If you need to ensure uniqueness across several columns, for example in tables where it takes more than one column to uniquely identify a row, then you can concatenate the indices on those columns. This will speed retrieval if you name those columns first in the target list, in the order in which they occur in the concatenated index. The syntax is:

```
CREATE UNIQUE INDEX <index_name>
ON  <table_name>
    (<column1_name, column2_name, ..., columnN_name>);
```

where the column names are those you want concatenated. This will speed retrieval on queries combining those same columns, in that same order, in the WHERE clause, such as:

```
WHERE   <column1_name> = <'constant'>
AND     <column2_name> = <'constant'>
AND     <columnN_name> = <'constant'>;
```

The two main ways of accessing data are: using a full table scan and using an index. Using an index will usually result in better performance than a full table scan because most SQL statements are set up to retrieve only a few specified rows of a table. However, if the retrieval consists of a large portion of the table, using the index will only increase the overhead.

Optimizing queries

While the ORACLE RDBMS will determine the access paths, you can influence its choice by the construction of your SQL query. Because there are usually several different ways to write a SQL query, the following points should be used as guidelines:

- An index will not be used if there is no WHERE clause in the statement
- If the WHERE clause contains either IS NULL or IS NOT NULL, an index will not be used
- Indices are more likely to be used on columns defined as NOT NULL
- A column defined as UNIQUE and NOT NULL fulfills the requirements for a key and therefore an index on it can enhance performance

In general, system optimizers will process non-nested queries (queries not containing subqueries) more efficiently than they will nested queries. (See the entry for W. Kim in the Bibliography for more information on non-nested queries.)

Summary

This chapter elaborates on the many practical uses of views in actually working with a database. It also shows that the way you form your SQL query can affect the performance of the system. It suggests ways to optimize performance by the judicious use of indices and the selective formation of your queries.

Chapter 11 exercises

Assume that you have an Employees table, a Customer table and a Suppliers table in the following exercises.

11.1 Create a view of the Employees table showing employee name, Social Security Number, and title for all employees who are not salesmen.
11.2 Create a view showing the average annual commission received by each salesman.
11.3 Create a view showing the total commission received by each salesman.
11.4 Can the view created in exercise 11.2 be updated?
11.5 Create a view of salesmen and the companies they service.
11.6 Can you insert a new row into the view you set up in exercise 11.1?
11.7 Can you delete a row from the view created in exercise 11.5?
11.8 Create a view showing the annual salary of all employees (from the base table showing monthly salaries).
11.9 Can you update the view created in exercise 11.8?
11.10 Can you delete a row from the view created in exercise 11.8?

Answers to chapter 11 exercises

11.1
```
CREATE VIEW non_sales
AS  SELECT  *
    FROM    Employees
    WHERE   NOT title = 'salesman';
```

The above WHERE clause could be entered as:

```
WHERE title <> 'salesman';)
```

11.2
```
CREATE VIEW salesmen
AS  SELECT  AVG(commission*12)
```

```
        FROM     Employees
        WHERE    title = 'salesman';
```

11.3
```
CREATE VIEW salesmen
AS   SELECT   SUM(commission)
     FROM     Employees
     WHERE    title = 'salesman';
```

11.4 No, because it contains a column based on an aggregate function.

11.5
```
CREATE VIEW clients
AS   SELECT   salesman_name, customer_name
     FROM     Employees, Customers
     WHERE    employee.title = 'salesmen'
     AND      salesman.district = customer.district;
```

11.6 Yes.

11.7 No, because it is derived from more than one table.

11.8
```
CREATE VIEW annual_salary
AS   SELECT   employee_name,(salary*12)
     FROM     Employees
     GROUP BY salesman;
```

11.9 No, because it contains a column based on an arithmetic expression.

11.10 Yes.

12 CHAPTER

Embedded SQL

This chapter presents a method for writing programs using the C programming language with embedded SQL statements to manipulate the data in an ORACLE database. Oracle Corporation provides a precompiler and a set of library functions to convert SQL statements into C code. This converted C code can then be compiled with an ordinary C compiler using the library provided by Oracle Corporation.

This method differs from PL/SQL, treated in a different chapter, in that it does not have the full functionality of PL/SQL. However, anything that you can achieve in PL/SQL you also can achieve in embedded SQL. Therefore, the choice is yours. If you prefer to use the C language without the special features of PL/SQL you can do so. Because some of you might have earlier versions of ORACLE, which do not include PL/SQL but do include PRO*C, you can follow the methods in this chapter to write programs with embedded SQL.

How the precompiler recognizes code to modify

All of the SQL statements that you use in embedded SQL must be preceded by the two words EXEC SQL. For example:

```
EXEC SQL UPDATE ......
```

For variables that the precompiler recognizes, you must include an EXEC SQL DECLARE section.

To include files that the precompiler must look at, use the following statement:

```
EXEC SQL INCLUDE <filename>
```

The precompiler will scan the file for useful information and then replace the EXEC SQL INCLUDE with #include, which your C compiler will recognize.

The variable declare section

To declare variables that the precompiler will recognize you must use the format:

```
EXEC SQL BEGIN DECLARE SECTION;
<variables>
EXEC SQL END DECLARE SECTION;
```

ORACLE uses a pseudo-type, VARCHAR, for character variables. For example:

```
EXEC SQL BEGIN DECLARE SECTION;
VARCHAR name[20];
int ssno;
EXEC SQL END DECLARE SECTION;
```

The above VARCHAR is equivalent to:

```
struct {
unsigned short len;
char arr[20];
}name;
```

Such variables are not set to null-terminated strings by ORACLE. Thus, for example:

```
EXEC SQL SELECT NAME INTO :name FROM EMP WHERE EMPNO = '10';
```

will result in the employee's name, whose employee number is 10, being selected into the arr portion of the VARCHAR name. If the employee's name is SMITH, the first five positions of name.arr will contain SMITH and name.len will contain the number five. Note that SMITH will not be null terminated in name.arr, but will probably be padded with blanks. Similarly, when using a VARCHAR for input, you should pad the character string with blanks and set the len variable. Note that variables declared in the declare section must be preceded by a colon (:) when they are used in a SQL statement.

You also can use ordinary char variables such as:

```
char name[25];
```

but they must be padded with blanks. Check the documentation for the version of PRO*C that you are using.

SQLCA

There is an include file that comes with ORACLE that contains the SQLCA. In order to include the SQLCA in your program, you need to use the line:

```
EXEC SQL INCLUDE SQLCA;
```

To include this file, ORACLE must know what is meant. In the case of VMS this involves a logical name SQLCA that must be properly set. For other systems, check your ORACLE documentation.

The SQLCA contains a struct, sqlca, in which ORACLE places important information that you need to program with embedded SQL. The most important member of sqlca is the integer sqlcode, which contains an indicator of the success or failure of an embedded SQL statement immediately after the statement is executed. If the value is zero, the SQL statement succeeded. If the value is negative, an error occurred. In that event, you will need to check your ORACLE error messages. A value of 1403 indicates row not found or nothing returned. This is useful for checking for the last row of a cursor. See cursors below.

Another member of sqlca is sqlca.sqlwarn[8], which is a CHAR array of warning flags. If sqlwarn[0] is set to 'W', then one of the other flags is set and some warning has occurred.

Logging in

In order to use embedded SQL in ORACLE, you will need to login. This is accomplished by the following statement:

```
EXEC SQL CONNECT :<user name> IDENTIFIED BY :<password>;
```

where <user name> is a CHAR variable of length 20 containing the user name and, possibly, a database identifier. And <password> is a string of length 20 containing the user's password. For example if:

```
char user_name[20] = "JONES";
char passwd[20] = "CAREY";
```

then,

```
EXEC SQL CONNECT :user_name IDENTIFIED BY :passwd;
```

should succeed in connecting you to the database.

Simple SQL statements in embedded SQL

The simplest statements to use in embedded SQL are INSERT, UPDATE, and DELETE. You can either use actual values as in:

```
EXEC SQL UPDATE SAL SET SALARY = SALARY + .05 * SALARY;
```

or you can use variables declared in the DECLARE section as in:

```
EXEC SQL UPDATE SAL SET SALARY = SALARY + :pct * SALARY;
```

where pct is a float declared in the declare section.

Arrays are allowed in SQL statements by ORACLE embedded SQL but we recommend using a for or a while loop, transferring the values to declared variables as in:

```
for(i = 0;i < lim;i++) {
    newsal = value[i];
    strcpy(name,name_value[i]);
    EXEC SQL UPDATE SAL SET SALARY = :newsal
    WHERE EMP = :name;
}
EXEC SQL COMMIT WORK RELEASE;
```

where newsal and name are variables declared in the declare section. The EXEC SQL COMMIT WORK RELEASE commits your changes to the database and logs you out. The word WORK is optional.

A similar for loop will handle an insert, delete or select as in the following examples:

```
for(i = 0;i < lim;i++) {
    newsal = value[i];
    strcpy(name,name_value[i]);
    EXEC SQL INSERT INTO SAL (SALARY,EMP)
    VALUES (:newsal,:name);
}
EXEC SQL COMMIT WORK RELEASE;
for(i = 0;i < lim;i++) {
    strcpy(name,name_value[i]);
    EXEC SQL DELETE FROM SAL
    WHERE EMP = :name;
}
EXEC SQL COMMIT WORK RELEASE;
for(i = 0;i < lim;i++) {
    strcpy(name,name_value[i]);
    EXEC SQL SELECT SALARY INTO :newsal
    WHERE EMP = :name;
```

```
        value[i] = value;
    }
```

Cursors

Cursors are the lifeblood of embedded SQL. They provide you with a way to handle a result table one row at a time inside a procedural language, such as, in our examples, the C programming language.

A *cursor* is a cursor for some given SELECT statement that produces a result table. Any SELECT statement can be the SELECT statement for a cursor. As you fetch the rows of the result table, one at a time, you can examine them and decide to update them providing the SELECT statement satisfies certain rules.

In general, a cursor can be used to update rows providing the SELECT statement does not involve more than one table and does not contain an ORDER BY clause. You should check the documentation of your version of PRO*C for any variation on these rules.

To use a cursor you must declare it, open it, establish a loop to fetch the rows in the result table, and then close it. As you fetch the rows you might want to update them. For example:

```
EXEC SQL BEGIN DECLARE SECTION;
char name[20];
float value;
EXEC SQL END DECLARE SECTION;
EXEC SQL DECLARE GET_SAL CURSOR FOR
SELECT EMP,SALARY FROM SAL;
EXEC SQL OPEN GET_SAL;
while(1) {
    EXEC SQL FETCH GET_SAL INTO :name,:value;
    if(sqlca.sqlcode == 1403) break;
}
EXEC SQL CLOSE GET_SAL;
```

This might seem slightly useless. Suppose you want to give employees a five percent raise if they make less than $1000 a month. The following code will do that:

```
EXEC SQL BEGIN DECLARE SECTION;
char name[20];
float value;
EXEC SQL END DECLARE SECTION;
EXEC SQL DECLARE GET_SAL CURSOR FOR
SELECT EMP,SALARY FROM SAL
FOR UPDATE OF SALARY;
EXEC SQL OPEN GET_SAL;
```

```
while(1) {
    EXEC SQL FETCH GET_SAL INTO :name,:value;
    if(sqlca.sqlcode = = 1403) break;
    if(value < 1000.00)
    EXEC SQL UPDATE SAL SET SALARY = 1.05 * value
        WHERE CURRENT OF GET_SAL;
}
EXEC SQL CLOSE GET_SAL;
EXEC SQL COMMIT WORK RELEASE;
```

The same thing could be accomplished more simply by the single embedded UPDATE statement:

```
EXEC SQL UPDATE SAL SET SALARY = 1.05 * SALARY
WHERE SALARY < 1000.00;
EXEC SQL COMMIT WORK RELEASE;
```

Cursors are necessary only when individual judgments have to be made on the individual rows or when an array has to be created containing the result table (possibly to be passed to a calling routine). For example:

```
EXEC SQL BEGIN DECLARE SECTION;
char name[20];
float value,pct;
EXEC SQL END DECLARE SECTION;
EXEC SQL DECLARE GET_SAL CURSOR FOR
SELECT EMP,SALARY FROM SAL;
EXEC SQL OPEN GET_SAL;
while(1) {
    EXEC SQL FETCH GET_SAL INTO :name,:value;
    if(sqlca.sqlcode = = 1403) break;
    printf("\nPercent increase for %s with salary %f > ",
    name,value);
    scanf("%f",&pct);
    pct /= 100;
    EXEC SQL UPDATE SAL SET SALARY = (1.0 + pct) * SALARY
    WHERE CURRENT OF GET_SAL;
}
EXEC SQL CLOSE GET_SAL;
EXEC SQL COMMIT WORK RELEASE;
```

Because cursors are commonly used to copy values into an array from a result table, ORACLE provides a special format for it:

```
EXEC SQL BEGIN DECLARE SECTION;
char name[500][20];
float value[500];
EXEC SQL END DECLARE SECTION;
```

```
EXEC SQL DECLARE GET_SAL CURSOR FOR
SELECT EMP,SALARY FROM SAL;
EXEC SQL OPEN GET_SAL;
EXEC SQL WHENEVER NOT FOUND GOTO finish
EXEC SQL FETCH GET_SAL INTO :name,:value;
finish:
```

This will fetch 500 rows unless there are not that many in the result table. The WHENEVER NOT FOUND GOTO could have been used in the previous examples instead of checking the value of sqlca.sqlcode. Besides NOT FOUND, WHENEVER allows the use of SQLERROR and SQLWARNING. Besides GOTO you may use STOP and CONTINUE. A SQLERROR occurs when sqlca.sqlcode is negative. A SQLWARNING occurs when sqlca.warn[0] is set to W. NOTFOUND is equivalent to sqlca.sqlcode = 1403. STOP causes a rollback followed by an exit. CONTINUE ignores the SQLWARNING.

If there are more than 500 rows in the result table, you can put the fetch into a while loop as follows:

```
EXEC SQL BEGIN DECLARE SECTION;
char name[500][20];
float value[500];
EXEC SQL END DECLARE SECTION;
EXEC SQL DECLARE GET_SAL CURSOR FOR
SELECT EMP,SALARY FROM SAL;
EXEC SQL OPEN GET_SAL;
while(1) {
    EXEC SQL WHENEVER NOT FOUND GOTO finish
    EXEC SQL FETCH GET_SAL INTO :name,:value;
    /*Add some lines of code here to dispose of each batch of 500*/
}
finish:
```

Error handling

ORACLE also uses the WHENEVER...GOTO construct for error handling. You can include an:

```
EXEC SQL WHENEVER SQLERROR GOTO <label>
```

in your while or for loop. At the label you can test the value of sqlca.sqlcode to find the error number and act appropriately. For example:

```
EXEC SQL BEGIN DECLARE SECTION;
char name[20];
float value,pct;
EXEC SQL END DECLARE SECTION;
EXEC SQL DECLARE GET_SAL CURSOR FOR
```

```
     SELECT EMP,SALARY FROM SAL;
     EXEC SQL OPEN GET_SAL;
     EXEC SQL WHENEVER SQLERROR GOTO err;
     while(1) {
          EXEC SQL FETCH GET_SAL INTO :name,:value;
          if(sqlca.sqlcode = = 1403) break;
          printf("\nPercent increase for %s with salary %f > ",
          name,value);
          scanf("%f",&pct);
          pct /= 100;
          EXEC SQL UPDATE SAL SET SALARY = (1.0 + pct) * SALARY
          WHERE CURRENT OF GET_SAL;
     }
     EXEC SQL CLOSE GET_SAL;
     EXEC SQL COMMIT WORK RELEASE;
     exit(0);
err:
     EXEC SQL ROLLBACK WORK RELEASE;
     printf("Program terminated with SQL error %d\n",
     sqlca.sqlcode);
     exit(1);
```

The EXEC SQL ROLLBACK WORK RELEASE statement eliminates all the changes you have made and logs you out of ORACLE. You might not want to do this. You might want to try some sort of recovery or just commit the changes you have made so you won't have to repeat them.

Indicator variables and NULL values

If a value in a table is NULL and you select it by means of a cursor or a single select, you can tell that it is NULL by using an indicator variable. An *indicator variable* is a short variable appended to the regular variable following a colon. If the value of the indicator variable is set to 0, the value is not null and has not been truncated before being inserted into the host variable. If the indicator variable is set to -1, the returned value is NULL. If the indicator variable is set to some positive value, the returned variable has been truncated and the value of the indicator variable is the length of the value before it was truncated. For example:

```
EXEC SQL BEGIN DECLARE SECTION;
char name[10];
short iname;
EXEC SQL END DECLARE SECTION;
EXEC SQL SELECT ENAME INTO :name:iname FROM EMP
WHERE EMPNO = 1345;
```

If iname is 0, the name selected is not null and has not been truncated. If iname is -1, there is a row with EMPNO = 1345 but, the name in that row is NULL. If iname is 15 the name selected is of length 15 but has been truncated to fit in the variable name.

The SQLCA structure

The structure sqlca that you include in your source file with the EXEC SQL INCLUDE SQLCA; command varies with the version of ORACLE that you have. In this section we will assume version 5.1, in which sqlca has the following structure:

```
struct sqlca {
char sqlcaid[8];
long sqlcabc;
long sqlcode;
struct {
    unsigned short sqlerrm1;
    char sqlerrmc[70];
} sqlerrm;
char sqlerrp[8];
long sqlerrd[6];
char sqlwarn[8];
char sqlext[8];
} sqlca;
```

Other than sqlcode, the most important other parts are sqlca.sqlerrm.sqlerrmc and sqlca.sqlwarn. sqlca.sqlerrm.sqlerrmc is the actual text of the error corresponding to the number in sqlcode. You can use this to actually print out the error message.

In the version under discussion, sqlwarn is an eight-character char. Its members have the following functions:

0: If set to 'W' indicates one of the other parts was set. Otherwise no warning occurred.

1: If set to 'W', one or more character data were truncated because the host variable was not wide enough.

2: If set to 'W' it indicates that a NULL value was ignored in the computation of a function, such as AVG.

3: If set to 'W' it indicates that the number of items in the target list does not equal the number of host variables provided to receive them.

4: If set to 'W' either an UPDATE or DELETE command has occurred without a WHERE clause.

5: Unused in the version under consideration.

6: Set to 'W' if the last statement executed causes ORACLE to rollback; possibly due to deadlock.

7: Set to 'W' if a row's data has been changed since the time the query started and the time the row was fetched.

Summary

Embedded SQL is a language that can be embedded in a host language to allow procedural programs to access a database. This chapter briefly covers what you need to know to write embedded SQL programs for the ORACLE database where the host language is the C programming language.

13
CHAPTER

PL/SQL

PL/SQL is a procedural programming language for use with the ORACLE RDBMS. It contains part of ORACLE's version of SQL as a sublanguage. If you are familiar with the programming language Pascal, you will notice PL/SQL is similar to Pascal because it is block structured and uses the same commands, BEGIN and END, to delimit the blocks. If you are familiar with the C programming language, which is block structured, you will see many similarities between C and PL/SQL.

If you have never worked with a block structured programming language, a *block* is a collection of programming commands that is delimited in some way at the beginning and end. C uses { and }. And both Pascal and PL/SQL use BEGIN and END. PL/SQL uses DECLARE to indicate that variables are about to be declared. If DECLARE immediately precedes BEGIN, then the variables declared are understood to be within the block begun by that BEGIN statement.

In PL/SQL you can define exceptions, which are described in detail later in this chapter, to handle errors that occur during the execution of the block. Exceptions are declared in the DECLARE portion of the block; then at the end of the block, you place the keyword EXCEPTION followed by <exception handlers>. Thus your block looks like:

```
DECLARE
    <declarations>
```

```
BEGIN
     <lines of code>
EXCEPTION
     <exception handlers>
END;
```

Subblocks, if there are any, are inserted between BEGIN and EXCEPTION. Blocks can be nested within other blocks. If a variable is defined within a block, it is not recognized outside the block. However, inner blocks do recognize variables defined in blocks that contain them. A variable defined in a block is *local* with respect to that block and *global* with respect to blocks nested within that block.

There are four ways to use PL/SQL. You can:

1. Embed PL/SQL blocks in the ORACLE Pro* languages
2. Use PL/SQL blocks in SQL*Forms
3. Run PL/SQL blocks from SQL*Plus
4. Run PL/SQL blocks from SQL*DBA

This chapter explains flow control commands of PL/SQL; SQL in PL/SQL, including the use of cursors; transaction processing; and SQL functions.

Delimiters and identifiers

PL/SQL has the following delimiters:

<table>
<tr><td>()</td><td></td></tr>
<tr><td>+,−,*,/,<,>,=</td><td>Plus, minus, times, divides, less than, greater than, and equals</td></tr>
<tr><td>**</td><td>Exponentiation</td></tr>
<tr><td>;</td><td>Terminates PL/SQL statements</td></tr>
<tr><td>.</td><td>Used to reference a column value with record variables</td></tr>
<tr><td>:</td><td>Signifies use of a host variable</td></tr>
<tr><td>'</td><td>Delimits a character string</td></tr>
<tr><td>"</td><td>Allows a character string to be an identifier</td></tr>
<tr><td>|</td><td>Used to denote or in exception handlers</td></tr>
<tr><td>:=</td><td>Variable assignment</td></tr>
<tr><td>||</td><td>String concatenation</td></tr>
<tr><td><<>></td><td>Delimits a loop name or a GOTO statement label</td></tr>
</table>

Identifiers in PL/SQL must be less than or equal to 30 characters in length; begin with a letter; and may contain up to 29 other letters, numbers or any of the characters $_#.

Flow of control

There are four kinds of flow of control statements in PL/SQL. They are:

1. IF...THEN, ELSEIF...THEN, ELSE, END IF
2. LOOPS
   A. LOOP, ENDLOOP
   B. FOR...LOOP, ENDLOOP
   C. WHILE...LOOP, ENDLOOP
3. GOTO
4. RAISE

These control sections are discussed in the following sections.

IF statements

The simplest form of the IF statement is:

```
IF <condition> THEN
   <lines of code>
END IF;
```

If the condition evaluates to true, then the lines of code are performed and control is transferred to the first statement after the END IF;. If the condition evaluates to false, control is transferred to the first statement after the END IF; without performing the lines of code.

ELSE IF...THEN can be used to test for other conditions and ELSE can be used to perform some other code in the event that none of the conditions holds true. For example:

```
IF        <condition 1> THEN
          <lines of code 1>
ELSEIF    <condition 2> THEN
          <lines of code 2>
ELSEIF    <condition 3> THEN
          <lines of code 3>
ELSE
          <lines of code 4>
END IF;
```

If <condition 1> holds true, <lines of code 1> will be performed. If <condition 1> is not true and <condition 2> is true, then <lines of code 2> will be performed. If <condition 1> and <condition 2> are not true and <condition 3> is true, <lines of code 3> will be performed. If <condition 1>, <condition 2>, and <condition 3> are false, then <lines of code 4> will be performed.

Loops

Loops are used to repeatedly perform code within a loop. For example:

```
LOOP
    <lines of code>
END LOOP;
```

will result in the lines of code within the loop being endlessly repeated. Because this is not a desirable state of affairs, there has to be a way to get out of the loop. PL/SQL provides the EXIT command to get out of the loop. For example:

```
LOOP
      <lines of code>
IF    <condition> THEN EXIT;
END LOOP;
```

will jump out of the loop after performing the lines of code whenever the condition is true. GOTO and RAISE also jump out of the loop.

One way to control a loop is to have an integer confined to a set of values that increases each time the loop is performed. When the integer increases to a value outside the set of values, the loop ends and control is transferred to the first statement after the loop. PL/SQL provides the command:

```
FOR <variable> IN <beginning of range>...<end of range> LOOP
```

for this purpose. For example:

```
FOR i IN 1..10 LOOP
<lines of code>
END LOOP;
```

will repeat the lines of code ten times. The first time i will have the value one, and the last time i will have the value ten. Each time through the loop i will be incremented by one.

The keyword REVERSE is provided to perform the loop with a decreasing variable. For example:

```
FOR i IN REVERSE 1..10 LOOP
<lines of code>
END LOOP;
```

will repeat the lines of code ten times. The first time i will have the value ten and the last time i will have the value one. Each time the loop is performed i will be decremented by one.

WHILE loops are provided to perform code repeatedly while a condition holds true. The format for a WHILE loop is:

```
WHILE <condition> LOOP
<lines of code>
END LOOP;
```

GOTO statements allow you to jump around in a block. You place a label somewhere in the block, and then GOTO followed by the label name causes control to jump to the first command following the label. For example:

```
WHILE <condition> LOOP
<lines of code 1>
IF <condition>
    GOTO gronk;
END IF;
END LOOP;
<<gronk>>
<lines of code 2>
```

If you are in the WHILE loop and the <condition> holds when you get to the IF statement, control will jump to the first statement in <lines of code 2>. Labels must be delimited by << and >>. You cannot jump into a loop by means of a GOTO. Using GOTO commands is poor programming practice and can make it extremely difficult to debug. The worst case is when the label precedes the GOTO. You can usually use some other means such as EXIT to get out of a loop and then follow the loop with an IF to determine what to do. It is beyond the scope of this book to discuss the principles of good programming practice but, we suggest that you never use a GOTO unless you cannot figure out another way to do what you want to do.

Cursors

The word *cursor* as used in this section does not refer to the cursor on your screen. A *cursor* is a data structure that allows you to procedurally work with a table that is the result of a SQL SELECT statement. By using a cursor you can access the rows of a result table one by one and do what you wish with the values in the columns.

In PL/SQL there are two kinds of cursors: *explicit* and *implicit*. If you intend to use an explicit cursor you must create it by declaring it in the declare section of a block. The format for this is:

```
CURSOR <cursor name> <parameter name> <parameter type> ...
    IS <select statement> FOR UPDATE OF <column name> ...;
```

where:

<cursor name> is the name by which you will reference the cursor. It must satisfy the requirements for identifiers.

<parameter name> is optional and there can be more than one parameter. The parameter(s) are to be used in the where clause of the SELECT statement. The parameter name can only be, and must be used in the SELECT statement in the cursor definition. The parameters will have values assigned to them in the OPEN statement. (See the upcoming section.)

<parameter type> can be CHAR, NUMBER, DATE, or BOOLEAN. No restrictions are added to the type. For example, just use CHAR, but not CHAR(10).

FOR UPDATE OF is used only if you intend to update a column or columns. If you do, you must list those columns after FOR UPDATE OF separated by commas.

To use a cursor, you must open it. The OPEN command evaluates the SELECT statement in the cursor definition using the values for the parameters supplied by the OPEN statement. The values for the parameters can be supplied using either *positional association* or *named association*. The result is a table that you can loop through row by row.

Using *positional association*, the format for the OPEN statement is:

```
OPEN <cursor name>(<parameter value>,...);
```

where:

<cursor name> must be the name assigned to the cursor in the CURSOR statement.

<parameter value> is a value to be supplied for the parameter occurring in the same position in the CURSOR statement.

Using *named association*, the format for the OPEN statement is:

```
OPEN <cursor name>(<parameter name> => <parameter value>,...);
```

where:

<cursor name> must be the name assigned to the cursor in the CURSOR statement.

<parameter name> is the name of a parameter occurring in the CURSOR statement.

<parameter value> is a value to be supplied for that parameter.

A cursor can be reopened without closing it. You might want to do this to change the parameter values. Once you have opened the cursor, there are two ways to step through the rows of the cursor. One way is to use a CURSOR FOR loop to be described below. The other way is to use the FETCH command. The FETCH command has the format:

```
FETCH <cursor name> INTO <variable name 1>,...,<variable name n>;
```

where:

<cursor name> is the name of the cursor in the cursor statement.

<variable name n> is the name of a declared variable. There must be as many variable names as there are columns in the result table of the CURSOR SELECT statement. The value in the current row, first column will be entered in <variable name 1>, and so on.

The FETCH statement also can be used with a record variable type. To declare a record variable for the cursor, you must declare a variable name following the CURSOR statement followed by the cursor name, followed by the expression %ROWTYPE. For example:

```
DECLARE
CURSOR gronk IS ...;
gronk_record      gronk%ROWTYPE;
```

declares gronk_record to be a record variable for the result table for the SELECT statement for the cursor gronk. Now you can use gronk_record in the FETCH statement as follows:

```
FETCH gronk INTO gronk_record;
```

The value for a given column of a row fetched into a record type variable can be accessed by using the name of the record type variable followed by a period followed by the column name of the column you want to access. For example, if you want to access id, you write gronk_record.id.

If you use ordinary variables in your FETCH statement, they must have been declared in the declare section of the block. ORACLE provides the %TYPE attribute to make sure that these variables have the same type as the columns that are fetched into them. The way to use this attribute is to write the variable name followed by the column name, followed immediately by %TYPE. For example:

```
DECLARE
employee_first_name      emp.first_name%TYPE
```

will ensure that the variable employee_first_name has the same datatype as the column first_name in the emp table.

When a cursor is opened, a cursor pointer is set to point before the first row of the result table. Each time the FETCH command is used it advances the cursor pointer one row further in the result table. If a fetch is performed when the cursor pointer is pointing at the last row, the cursor pointer will be advanced beyond the end of the result table. If you want to reset the cursor pointer back before the beginning of the result table, you can reopen the cursor without closing it, using the same parameter values.

When you have finished with an opened cursor, you can close the cursor. The format for that is:

```
CLOSE <cursor name>;
```

CLOSE releases any resources held by an opened cursor.

You will normally use the FETCH command in a loop to cause the cursor pointer to step through the rows of the result table. If there are no parameters in the CURSOR SELECT statement, then ORACLE provides a CURSOR FOR loop to allow you to step through the rows of the result table without opening the cursor, and without the FETCH command. The format for that is:

```
FOR <record variable name> IN <cursor name> LOOP
<lines of code using record variable name dot column names>
END LOOP;
```

where:

<record variable name> is a name of a record variable declared by virtue of appearing in a FOR loop where IN is followed by a cursor name. This record variable is not declared in the declare section of the block. The first time through the loop, the cursor will be opened and the record variable will hold the values in the first row of the result table. On successive passes through the loop, the record variable will hold the values in successive rows. When the loop has completed the last row of the result table, the loop will be exited and the cursor will be closed.

<cursor name> is the name of a cursor previously declared in the block.

If your declaration of a cursor contains the clause FOR UPDATE OF, you can update the columns named after the FOR UPDATE OF clause in the current cursor row by using a SQL UPDATE statement with the key words WHERE CURRENT OF. The format for that is:

```
UPDATE <table name> SET <column name> = <SQL expression>,...
WHERE CURRENT OF <cursor name>;
```

Similarly, you can use the SQL DELETE command with WHERE CURRENT OF providing the cursor definition contains the words FOR UPDATE OF.

In the UPDATE command you can replace <SQL expression> with a SQL SELECT provided it returns only one value (one column and one row) and the value returned is of the same datatype as the column being updated.

For each SQL command not associated with a declared cursor (an explicit cursor), ORACLE opens a cursor (an implicit cursor). The most recently opened implicit cursor can be referenced by the cursor name SQL%.

Cursor attributes

There are four variables (ORACLE documentation calls them cursor attributes) cursor SQL statements: %NOTFOUND, %FOUND, %ROWCOUNT, and %ISOPEN.

%NOTFOUND and %FOUND are set to the logical values, true, false, and NULL by ORACLE. %FOUND has the value NULL before the first fetch. After each FETCH command, %FOUND has the value true if a row was returned, and false if not. If %FOUND has the value NULL, so does %NOTFOUND. If %FOUND is true, %NOTFOUND is false; and if %FOUND is false, then %NOTFOUND is true.

%ROWCOUNT contains the number of rows fetched from the cursor. Before the first row is fetched it has the value zero.

%ISOPEN is true if the cursor is open and false if it is closed.

To reference these variables, you use the cursor name immediately followed by the %variable name. In the case of implicit cursors you use the name SQL for the implicit cursor.

SQL%FOUND is true if an insert, update or delete affected one or more rows, or if a single row select returned a row. Otherwise, it is false.

SQL%ROWCOUNT has a value equal to the number of rows affected by the last SQL statement. Because an implicit cursor is always closed immediately after the associated SQL statement is executed, SQL%ISOPEN, when referenced, is always false.

SQL commands that do not require an explicit cursor

If you want to select where the result table has only one row, you can use the SELECT...INTO form of the SELECT statement. The format for SELECT ...INTO is:

```
SELECT <column 1,...,column n> INTO <variables or record variable>
    FROM <rest of SELECT>;
```

where:

<column 1,...,column n> is the column list.

<variables or record variable> is either a list of variables to be assigned the values retrieved or a single-record variable.

<rest of SELECT> is the rest of a normal SELECT statement.

If zero rows or more than one row is returned there will be an error. If zero rows are returned:

- SQLCODE returns −1403
- SQLERRM returns "no data found"

- The NO_DATA_FOUND exception is raised
- SQL%NOTFOUND is true
- SQL%FOUND is false
- SQL%ROWCOUNT is zero

If more than one row is returned:

- SQLCODE returns −2112
- SQLERRM returns "too many rows"
- The TOO_MANY_ROWS exception is raised
- SQL%NOTFOUND is false
- SQL%FOUND is true
- SQL%ROWCOUNT is two

For the format of the DELETE, UPDATE, and INSERT commands see chapter 8. If zero rows are affected:

- SQL%NOTFOUND is true
- SQL%FOUND is false
- SQL%ROWCOUNT is zero

If more than one row is affected:

- SQL%NOTFOUND is false
- SQL%FOUND is true
- SQL%ROWCOUNT is the number of rows affected

Indicator variables

If you are using a precompiler and you are retrieving database columns that might contain NULL values, you will need to use indicator variables. Similarly, if you are inserting NULL values into the database you will need to use indicator variables.

An *indicator variable* is an integer variable that must be defined in the Declare section as a two-byte integer. To use it, you follow the regular host variable with a colon and then the indicator variable. For example:

```
SELECT...INTO :name:name_ind...
```

or

```
INSERT INTO...VALUES (:name:name_ind,...
```

where name is a host variable and name_ind is a host variable used as an indicator variable.

If, after the execution of the SELECT or FETCH statements, the indicator variable has the value −1, then the value in the database is NULL. If the indicator variable is 0 the value is NOT NULL. If the value of the indicator variable is > 0, a truncated string was inserted into the host variable. The value of the indicator variable is the length of the string before it was inserted.

If you use an indicator variable with a value of −1 in an INSERT statement, a NULL value will be inserted into the database. Using an indicator variable with a value greater than 0 will cause the value of the host variable to be inserted into the database.

In PL/SQL you do not need to use indicator variables. You can test a host variable to see if it is NULL by using:

```
IF :name IS NULL THEN....
```

and you can assign a NULL value to a host variable with the following type of statement:

```
:name := NULL;
```

Exceptions

Exceptions are used in PL/SQL to handle any errors that occur during execution of a block. There are two types of exceptions, internally defined exceptions and user-defined exceptions. First let's look at user-defined exceptions.

User-defined exceptions

A user-defined exception must be declared in the Declare section of the block. The format for this is:

```
DECLARE
...
<exception name> EXCEPTION;
...
BEGIN
```

During the execution of the block, between the EXCEPTION and BEGIN statements, you must check, by means of an IF statement, for the occurrence of your user-defined exception. If your user-defined exception has occurred, you execute a RAISE statement to transfer control to the exception handler in the Exception section of the block. The (picture) situation is as follows:

```
DECLARE
    ...
    <exception name> EXCEPTION;
    ...
BEGIN
    ...
```

```
IF <exception condition>
    RAISE <exception name>;
END IF;
...

EXCEPTION
    ...
WHEN <exception name> =>
    <lines of code to process the exception>
...
OTHERS =>
    <lines of code to process any exception not explicitly mentioned after a
    WHEN>
END;
```

More than one exception can be processed by the same lines of code. To do this, write:

```
WHEN <exception name 1|...|exception name n> =>
```

The | can be read as "or." After the exception is processed, control passes to the first statement after the end of the block.

RAISE also can occur within an exception handler without the exception name. This causes PL/SQL to search for an exception handler with the same name in the enclosing block. If such an exception handler is not found in the enclosing block, the search is repeated in the block enclosing the enclosing block. Finally, if no exception handler is found, PL/SQL stops execution with an unhandled exception error.

Internally defined exceptions

Besides the user-defined exceptions, ORACLE has 13 internally defined exceptions:

1. DUP_VAL_ON_INDEX
   An index that was specified as unique has duplicate keys. (ORACLE error number -0001)
2. INVALID_CURSOR
   A cursor operation is illegal. For example, closing an unopened cursor. (ORACLE error number -1001)
3. INVALID_NUMBER
   A conversion of a character string to a number has failed. (ORACLE error number -1722)
4. LOGIN_DENIED
   An invalid user name or password has been entered. (ORACLE error number -1017)

5. NO_DATA_FOUND
   A SELECT statement has returned zero rows. (ORACLE error number +100)
6. NOT_LOGGED_ON
   PL/SQL has issued an ORACLE call without being logged on. (ORACLE error number −1012)
7. PROGRAM_ERROR
   PL/SQL has an internal problem. (ORACLE error number −6501)
8. STORAGE_ERROR
   PL/SQL has run out of memory or memory is corrupted. (ORACLE error number −6500)
9. TIMEOUT_ON_RESOURCE
   Timeout has occurred while ORACLE is waiting for a resource. (ORACLE error number −0051)
10. TOO_MANY_ROWS
   A SELECT statement returns more than one row. (ORACLE error number −2112)
11. TRANSACTION_BACKED_OUT
   ORACLE has backed out of a transaction because of a processing error. (ORACLE error number −0061)
12. VALUE_ERROR
   Catchall for conversion and constraint errors. (ORACLE error number −6502)
13. ZERO_DIVIDE
   You attempted to divide by zero. (ORACLE error number −1476)

To use these internal exceptions with a name, you must declare the name for the exception in the Declare section of the block. Then, you must tie the name to the ORACLE error number. The format for this is:

```
DECLARE
    <internal exception name> EXCEPTION;
    PRAGMA EXCEPTION_INIT(<internal exception name>,<error code>);
BEGIN
    ...
EXCEPTION
    WHEN <internal exception name> =>
        <lines of error handling code>
END;
```

An example of a specific case is:

```
DECLARE
    TOO_MANY_ROWS EXCEPTION;
    PRAGMA EXCEPTION_INIT(TOO_MANY_ROWS, -2112);
BEGIN
    ...
    SELECT ...
    ...
EXCEPTION
    WHEN TOO_MANY_ROWS =>
    <take care of the error>
END;
```

The keyword PRAGMA means that the statement conveys information to the PL/SQL compiler—rather than being processed.

Transactions in PL/SQL

In order to avoid corruption of your database, you must frequently make a number of changes simultaneously. For example, if you make a sale, you need to enter the sale in the Sales table and update the Inventory table. If you perform just one of these actions and not the other, your database will be out of sync, corrupted.

In order to avoid corruption of your database, the concept of a transaction has been developed. For example, a transaction might include both entering a sale and updating inventory.

ORACLE has the commands COMMIT, ROLLBACK, and SAVEPOINT to help you to avoid corruption of your database. Between commits no actual changes are made to the database. When you perform a commit all of the changes since the last commit are actually made. If an error occurs, you can rollback the database to the state it was in after the previous commit. The SAVEPOINT command is provided so that you do not need to rollback all the way to the previous commit.

The format for the SAVEPOINT command is:

```
SAVEPOINT <savepoint identifier>;
```

where <savepoint identifier> is an identifier that you choose for the savepoint.

The format for the ROLLBACK statement is:

```
ROLLBACK [WORK] [TO [SAVEPOINT] <savepoint identifier>];
```

where:

[WORK] is an optional key word.

TO is optional to be used only if you want to identify a savepoint to rollback to. Any intervening savepoints will be erased.

[SAVEPOINT] is an optional keyword.

<savepoint identifier> is an identifier used previously in a SAVEPOINT command.

The format for COMMIT is:

COMMIT [WORK];

where [WORK] is an optional keyword.

The COMMIT command executes the changes you have made to the database. Before you perform a commit, any queries you make of the database will show the changes you have made but queries by others will not show those changes. The COMMIT command also releases any locks you have placed on the database. (See chapter 4 for more information about locks.)

The SET TRANSACTION command allows you to establish a read-only transaction. The format for that is:

SET TRANSACTION [READ ONLY];

where [READ ONLY] is optional. For more details about SET TRANSACTION see the *SQL Language Reference Manual.*

PL/SQL functions

There are six types of functions in PL/SQL. They are error reporting, character, numeric, date, data conversion, and miscellaneous. You can use := (assignment) with these functions to place the result in a variable.

Error-reporting functions

The error-reporting functions are SQLCODE and SQLERRM. SQLCODE returns the ORACLE error number of the last error that occurred.

The format for SQLERRM is:

SQLERRM[(<error_code>)]

where (<error code>) is optional and is any ORACLE error code. If (<error code>) is omitted the result is the same as if SQLERRM(SQLCODE) had been used.

Character functions

The following are the ORACLE SQL character functions:

ASCII(str char)	returns the ASCII code for the first character in the string.
CHR(number)	returns the character corresponding to the ASCII number.

INITCAP(string)	capitalizes the first letter of a string.
LENGTH(string)	returns the length of a character string.
LOWER(string)	changes all characters to lowercase in the string.
LPAD(string,length[,pad char])	left pads the string to length. If the optional [,pad char] is used, that character is used to pad the string.
LTRIM(string,set)	removes all characters in set from the left of string up to the first character not in set.
RPAD	same as LPAD except on the right.
RTRIM	same as LTRIM except on the right.
SUBSTR(string,position[,len])	returns the substring of string starting at position of length len. If len is omitted, returns to end.
UPPER(string)	convert all letters to uppercase.

Numeric functions

The following are the ORACLE SQL numeric functions:

ABS( )	is the absolute value.
CEIL(n)	is the smallest integer greater than or equal to n.
FLOOR(n)	largest integer less than or equal to n.
MOD(m,n)	remainder of m divided by n.
POWER(m,n)	is m to the nth power.
ROUND(m,n)	is m rounded to n decimal places. If n omitted, m rounded to zero decimal places.
SIGN(n)	returns the sign of n.
TRUNC(m,n)	is m truncated to n decimal places or zero decimal places if n is omitted.
SQRT(n)	is the square root if n is positive, otherwise it is NULL.

Date functions

The following are the ORACLE SQL date functions:

ADD_MONTHS(date,n)	is n months added to date. The variables date and n can be in reverse order.
LAST_DAY(date)	is the last day of the month.

MONTHS_BETWEEN(date1,date2)	is the number of months between date1 and date2.
NEW_TIME(date1,timezone1,timezone2)	reads a given date and time in the first time zone, timezone 1, and returns the date and time in the second time zone, time zone 2. Possible time zones are:

AST	Atlantic standard time
ADT	Atlantic daylight time
BST	Bering standard time
BDT	Bering daylight time
CST	Central standard time
CDT	Central daylight time
EST	Eastern standard time
EDT	Eastern daylight time
HST	Alaska-Hawaii standard time
HDT	Alaska-Hawaii daylight time
MST	Mountain standard time
MDT	Mountain daylight time
NST	Newfoundland standard time
PST	Pacific standard time
PDT	Pacific daylight time
YST	Yukon standard time
YDT	Yukon daylight time

NEXT_DAY(date,day name)	first date with day name later than date.
ROUND(date,format)	rounds date depending on format. If format is omitted DD is the default.

The possible formats are:

CC,SCC	century
SYYY,YYYY,YEAR SYEAR,YYY,YY,Y	year (rounds up to July 1)
Q	quarter (rounds up on 16th of 2nd month)
MONTH,MON,MM	month (rounds up on 16th)
WW	start of week of year
W	start of week of month
DDD,DD,J	day
DAY,DY,D	nearest Sunday
HH,HH12,HH24	hour
MI	minute

Conversion functions

The following are the ORACLE SQL conversion functions:

TO_CHAR(date,fmt)	converts date to character string. For formats see "Format Models" in the *SQL Language Reference Manual.*
TO_CHAR(n)	converts n to a character string.
TO_DATE(string,format)	converts character string to date.
TO_NUMBER(string)	converts a character string to a number.

Miscellaneous functions

The following is the miscellaneous function in ORACLE SQL:

NVL(arg1,arg2)	(The NVL = null value) takes two arguments of the same type and returns arg1 if it is not NULL. If arg1 is NULL, returns arg2.

Summary

PL/SQL is a programming language for application programming that first occurs in ORACLE version 6. In addition to SQL and CURSORS it contains procedural commands so that it can be used by itself rather than being embedded in a host language.

14
CHAPTER

Relational algebra and SQL

While SQL has been said to resemble tuple relational calculus, SQL also owes much to relational algebra. In this chapter we develop the relevant parts of relational algebra and give corresponding SQL queries to show the relationship between SQL and relational algebra.

Given a finite set of attributes $U = \{ A1, A2, \ldots, Au \}$ with domains dom(A i), a *relation scheme* is a subset of U. A *relational database scheme* D over U is a collection of relation schemes, $\{R1, R2, \ldots, Rd\}$, such that the union of the $R i$ is U. Given a relation scheme R, a tuple, t, over R is a single-valued mapping from the members of R to the domains of the members of R such that $t (A i)$ is a member of dom($A i$) for $A i$ a member of R. A relation over a relation scheme R is a finite set of tuples over R.

Relations over a relation scheme R are frequently displayed as rectangular tables where the column headings are the members of R and the rows are tuples such that, if t is a tuple, then $t (A i)$ is entered in the row corresponding to t and the column corresponding to $A i$.

Relational definitions

If $S1,S2,\ldots,Sk$ are sets then a tuple on $S1,S2,\ldots,Sk$ is an expression $(s1,s2,\ldots,s\,k)$ where si is a member of Si for $i = 1,2,\ldots,k$. The *Cartesian product* $S1 \times S2 \times \ldots \times Sk$ is the set of all such tuples. A tuple may also be thought of as a function f from the set labels $S1,S2,\ldots,Sk$ into the sets $S1,S2,\ldots,Sk$ such that the value of f at Si is a member of Si . Thus, if t is a tuple and A is an attribute, you can write $t[A]$ to denote the value of t at A. This notation is particularly useful in the case of a relation scheme R over the attributes $A1,A\,2,\ldots,Ak$. Then the members of a relation r over the scheme R are tuples over the $A\,i$'s.

Example

If $R = \{A,B,C\}$ where Dom(A) = Dom(B) = Dom(C) = the set of integers, and r is the relation:

A	*B*	*C*
1	1	1
2	3	1

then you may think of r as consisting of the tuples t and u where $t[A] = 1$, $t[B] = 1$, $t[C] = 1$, $u[A] = 2$, $u[B] = 3$, and $u[C] = 1$.

Boolean operators

The Boolean operators in relational algebra are union (∩), intersection (∩) and difference (−). These operators may only be applied between two relations having the same relation schemes. The *union* of two relations is the set of all tuples that are in either one. The *intersection* of two relations is the set of all tuples that are in both. And the *difference* of two relations is the set of all tuples that are in one but not the other.

Example

Let $r1$ and $r2$ be the two following relations:

r1			*r2*		
A	*B*	*C*	*A*	*B*	*C*
1	1	1	3	3	3
2	2	2	1	4	9
3	3	3	3	3	2

Then the union, $r1 \cap r2$, is:

A	*B*	*C*
1	1	1
2	2	2

A	*B*	*C*
3	3	3
1	4	9
3	3	2

The intersection, $r1 \cap r2$, is:

A	*B*	*C*
3	3	3

The difference, $r1 - r2$, is:

A	*B*	*C*
1	1	1
2	2	2

ORACLE SQL includes union, intersection, and difference. For example, to get the union here you could write:

```
SELECT    *
FROM      r1
UNION
SELECT    *
FROM      r2 ;
```

Projection operator

Given a relation *r* on relation scheme *R* , the projection, *s*, of *r* on some subset *S* of *R* is the restriction of the tuples in *R* to the members of *S*. You denote the projection on *S* by π *S* .

Example

Let *r* be the relation:

A	*B*	*C*
1	1	1
1	2	3
3	2	1

Then you have:

$\pi\{A,B\}r$

A	*B*
1	1
1	2
3	2

$\pi\{A,C\}r$

A	*C*
1	1
1	3
3	1

$\pi\{B\}r$

B
1
2

Repeated rows are removed. That is why $\pi\{B\}$ has only two rows. In SQL, projection is achieved by means of the target list, in other words, by selecting only those columns of the subscheme that you want.

Select operator

The select operator $\sigma A = a$ operates on a relation r to give the subrelation of those tuples t such that $t[A] = a$, for some constant value a.

Example

Let r be the relation:

A	*B*	*C*
1	1	2
1	2	1
2	3	2

Then $\sigma B = 1$ is:

A	*B*	*C*
1	1	2

The corresponding SQL query expression is:

```
SELECT    *
FROM      r
WHERE     B = 1;
```

Join operator

Given two relations $r1$ and $r2$ on relation schemes $R1$ and $R2$, you define the join of $r1$ and $r2$ to be a relation r on the union of $R1$ and $R2$. Namely, it is those tuples whose projection on $R1$ match some tuple of $r1$, and whose projection on $R2$ match some tuple of $r2$. The join of $r1$ and $r2$ is denoted $r1 \bowtie r2$.

Example

If $r1$ and $r2$ are the relations:

A	*B*	*C*	*D*	*B*	*D*	*E*
1	1	1	1	1	1	1
2	2	1	3	2	3	6
1	2	5	3	1	1	5
1	2	3	4	4	3	2

Then $r1 \bowtie r2$ is:

A	B	C	D	E
1	1	1	1	1
1	1	1	1	5
2	2	1	3	6
1	2	5	3	6

Notice that some rows in the original relations appear more than once in the join while others might not appear at all. The previous join may be written in SQL as follows:

```
SELECT   A,B,C,D,E
FROM     r1,r2
WHERE    r1.B = r2.B
AND      r1.D = r2.D
```

It is apparent, from the above SQL expression that the join is a special case of the equijoin. (See chapter 10 for a definition of an equijoin.) Relational algebra also has join operators involving other comparators than equals. These are called *theta joins*, (θ) and are defined exactly in the same way as the equijoin except that equals sign (=) is replaced with any of the following symbols: <, >, <=, >= or <>.

Division of relations, lossy joins

If you think of the join as a generalized multiplication for relations, then you would like to have an operator analogous to division. Let *r* be a relation over the scheme *R* and *s* be a relation over the scheme *S* where *S* is a subset of *R*. For each scheme *S'* such that *S* union *S'* equals *R*, you would like to find a relation *s'* such that *s* ÷ *s'* equals *r*. In general that is impossible.

Example 1

Let *r* and *s* be the relations:

r			*s*	
A	B	C	A	B
1	2	3	1	4

There is no relation on any subset of { *A,B,C* } that will join with *s* to produce *r*. That is because tuple in *r* is not the projection on { *A,B* } of any tuple in *s*.

In view of the above example, let's focus on division when *s* is the result of a projection operating on *r*.

Example 2

Let *r* be the relation shown below and let *s* and *s'* be π\{ *A,B* \}*r* and π *A,C* \}*r*, respectively:

r			*s*		*s'*	
A	*B*	*C*	*A*	*B*	*A*	*C*
1	2	3	1	2	1	3
1	3	4	1	3	1	4

Then $s \bowtie s'$ is:

$s \bowtie s'$		
A	*B*	*C*
1	2	3
1	2	4
1	3	3
1	3	4

Clearly, $s \bowtie s'$ contains the rows in *r* plus two additional rows and, therefore, is not equal to *r*. This is an example of a *lossy join*. The term "lossy join" is misleading because a lossy join always contains more rows than the original relation. If you repeat the operation by projecting on $\{A,B\}$ and $\{A,C\}$, and then join again, you get the relation $s \bowtie s'$ back again.

Thus, there is no easy way to define an operator analogous to division. In relational database literature (see, for example, the reference listed in the Bibliography under David Maier) the division operator is defined as follows:

Let *r* be a relation on the scheme *R* and s be a relation on the scheme S where S is a subset of *R*. Let $s' = r \div s$ be the largest relation on the scheme $R - S$ such that $s \bowtie s'$ is a subrelation of *r*. Because S and $R - S$ are disjoint, $s \bowtie s'$ is the Cartesian product of s and s'.

Example 3

Let *r* and s be the same as in the previous example. The r ÷ s is clearly the relation on $\{C\}$ which has no rows and is called the *empty relation*.

Division is frequently used in database queries to find objects that have certain properties. For example, if you have the relation scheme R = { *prisoner_name,charge* }, and you want to find those prisoners charged with DUI, the following query will get them.

```
SELECT    prisoner_name
FROM PRISONERS
WHERE     charge = 'DUI';
```

In effect, the above query divides any relation over *R* by the relation:

charge
'DUI'

Remarks

Both Maier and Yang have complete treatments of relational algebra. Codd defined relational algebra in a 1971 paper entitled "Relational Completeness of Data Base Sublanguage," giving the operators you have named here and defining relational completeness in terms of relational algebra. Date in his book *Relational Database: Selected Writings* outlines a proof that SQL is relationally complete—that every operation in relational algebra can be performed in SQL.

Summary

Relational definitions were given and Boolean operators were discussed, along with Projection, Select, and Join operators. Lossy joins were explained. For further information on these topics, the literature on relational algebra was cited.

Chapter 14 exercises

14.1 Let the relations *r*1 and *r*2 be:

*r*1		*r*2	
A	B	A	B
1	1	3	5
3	5	1	2
5	6	2	9

a. Find the union, intersection, and difference.
b. Write a SQL query expression for the union.
c. Write a SQL query expression for the intersection.
d. Write a SQL query expression for the difference.

14.2 Given a relation *r* over the relation scheme {*prisoner_name, charge*} let *s* be the relation:

charge
'DUI'
'ARSON'

Find a SQL expression for $r \div s$

14.3 Given the relations *r*, *s*, and *t* as follows:

r		*s*		*t*	
A	*B*	*B*	*C*	*C*	*A*
1	2	3	4	5	6
2	3	5	6	4	2

r		s		t	
A	B	B	C	C	A
1	2	3	1	1	2
7	8	2	4	4	1

Compute $(r \bowtie s) \bowtie t$ and show that it is the same as $r \bowtie (s \bowtie t)$.

14.4 Compute the join of *r* and *s* where *r* and *s* are:

r		s	
A	B	C	D
1	2	1	2
2	4	2	3

Answers to chapter 14 exercises

14.1a The union, intersection, and difference, in that order, are:

A	B	A	B	A	B
1	1	3	5	1	1
3	5	5	6		
5	6				
1	2				
2	9				

14.1b
```
SELECT    *
FROM      r1
UNION
SELECT    *
FROM      r2;
```

14.1c
```
SELECT    *
FROM      r1
WHERE EXISTS
(SELECT   *
FROM      r2
WHERE     r1.A = r2.A
AND       r1.B = r2.B);
```

14.1d
```
SELECT    *
FROM      r1
WHERE NOT EXISTS
(SELECT   *
FROM      r2
WHERE     r1.A = r2.A
AND       r1.B = r2.B);
```

14.2
```
SELECT    prisoner_name
FROM      R
```

```
WHERE    charge = 'DUI'
AND      charge = 'ARSON';
```

is wrong because there cannot be two charges in a single row. The following is one possible correct query using a subquery:

```
SELECT prisoner_name
FROM R
WHERE charge = 'DUI'
AND prisoner_name IN
(SELECT prisoner_name
FROM R
WHERE charge = 'ARSON');
```

14.3

A	*B*	*C*
1	2	4
2	3	4
2	3	1

14.4

A	*B*	*C*	*D*
1	2	1	2
1	2	2	3
2	4	1	2
2	4	2	3

This is the Cartesian product.

15

CHAPTER

Logic and SQL

Let's reconsider queries. What is a query? Suppose you have a database consisting of shipments of auto parts to various locations throughout the U.S. and you want to know what parts you shipped to the dealer in Cleveland on Thursday. You might like to ask the computer: "Give me a list of parts shipped to the dealer in Cleveland on Thursday." However, if you type that in you'll get nothing. The software available today is incapable of interpreting a simple request unless it is formulated in some fixed, limited "formal" language.

Because queries such as the one in the preceding paragraph contemplate a set of things (perhaps two left fenders and a brake shoe) as the answer, it is desirable for the formal language to be able to determine sets as answers.

First-order logic was developed by mathematicians in the first part of this century and the latter part of the previous century for the purpose of studying the foundations and consistency of mathematics. This was necessary at the time because mathematicians had been plagued by paradoxes. First-order logic aimed at developing a consistent set theory and, thus, contained a language for describing sets. (For a treatment of first-order logic see the references listed for Church or Mendelson in the Bibliography.)

The first-order logic for describing sets was ideal as a first step toward a query language for querying about sets. A part of it was first adopted by Codd in 1971 for queries on relational databases. Codd called his development the relational calculus, and called his queries alpha expressions. He then showed that alpha expressions could be converted to operations in the relational algebra. In the recent literature (see, for example, Maier and Yang) the relational calculus comes in two forms—*tuple relational calculus* and *domain relational calculus*. In tuple relational calculus the variables refer to tuples or rows in relations. In domain relational calculus the variables refer to attributes instead of rows. Codd's relational calculus is like tuple relational calculus.

This chapter contains a brief overview of the entire development starting with propositional calculus and ending with a slightly modified version of Codd's relational calculus. To show how SQL resembles tuple relational calculus, examples and exercises are given involving the creation of alpha expressions to represent queries, and the conversion of these alpha expressions to SQL.

Relational definitions

Given a finite set of attributes $U = \{A_1,A_2,\ldots,A_u\}$ with domains dom(A_i), a relation scheme is a subset of U. A relational database scheme D over U is a collection of relation schemes, $\{R_1,R_2,\ldots,R_d\}$, such that the union of the R_i is U. Given a relation scheme R, a tuple, t, over R is a single-valued mapping from the members of R to the domains of the members of R such that $t(A_i)$ is a member of dom(A_i) for A_i a member of R. A relation over a relation scheme R is a finite set of tuples over R.

Relations over a relation scheme R are frequently displayed as rectangular tables where the column headings are the members of R and the rows are tuples such that, if t is a tuple, then $t(A_i)$ is entered in the row corresponding to t and the column corresponding to A_i.

Example

If $R = \{A,B,C\}$ where Dom(A) = Dom(B) = Dom(C) = the set of integers, and r is the relation:

A	*B*	*C*
1	1	1
2	3	1

then, you might think of r as consisting of the tuples t and u where $t[A]$ = 1, $t[B]$ = 1, $t[C]$ = 1, $u[A]$ = 2, $u[B]$ = 3, and $u[C]$ = 1.

Formal theory

In mathematical logic an entity known as a *formal theory* is defined in the following way:

1. An infinite set of symbols S is given. A finite sequence of these symbols is called an *expression*.
2. Some expressions are called well-formed formulas (wfs). We will call a single well-formed formula a wff.
3. Some of the wfs are designated as axioms.
4. A finite set of "rules of inference" is given whereby some wfs can be derived from others. For example, "from A implies B and A you can derive B" is a rule of inference known as *modus ponens*.
5. A *proof* is a sequence of wfs where each wfs is either an axiom or can be derived from those preceding it by one of the rules of inference.
6. A *theorem* is the last member of a proof.

A query language only uses the first and second definitions. The rest are included here for completeness. In addition to these two definitions, a query language requires a well-defined *interpretation*.

Interpretations

Everyone is familiar with the idea of an interpretation. Frequently, after listening to someone speak you ask someone else what their interpretation is of what was said. Or you might ask "How do you interpret that?" If someone speaks of a cat you might think of a particular cat. That is another way of interpreting what they said. Another kind of interpretation is whether or not a statement is true or false (or plausible). A formal theory is given meaning by means of an interpretation without which it is simply a meaningless collection of sequences of symbols.

In mathematics, an *interpretation* is simply a function that maps the symbols in a formal theory to something else (which usually has more meaning). As you will see, the idea of an interpretation plays an important role in both first order logic and the relational calculus. Namely, the answer to a query is those rows of a relation for which the conditions of the query are interpreted to be true or satisfied. If you have a query language in which a particular query cannot be interpreted to be satisfied or not satisfied, then that query cannot be executed in the given query language.

Propositional calculus

The set of symbols in propositional calculus is as follows:

1. An infinite set of statement letters $A_i i = 1$ to infinity.
2. Three primitive connectives AND, OR, and NOT.
3. Right and left parentheses.

The rules for forming well-formed formulas (wfs) are:

1. All statement letters are wfs.
2. If *X* and *Y* are wfs then so are (NOT *X*), (*X* AND *Y*), and (*X* OR *Y*).

These rules may be repeated any number of times. For example, if *A* and *B* are statement letters, then *A* is a wff and *B* is a wff. Applying rule two you see that (NOT *A*) is a wff. Applying rule two again ((NOT *A*) AND *B*) is seen to be a wff and this can go on and on. This type of definition is said to be a *recursive definition*. All definitions in this chapter with rules will be understood to be recursive—the rules may be repeated an arbitrary number of times.

Frequently, in the logic literature, the rule, "Nothing else is a . . ." is added to the list of rules for recursive definitions. To avoid repeating this rule everywhere a recursive definition occurs, it should be understood that "Nothing else is a . . ." applies.

The main interpretation for propositional calculus is a set of mappings, called truth functions, from wfs to the set TF = {TRUE,FALSE}. Given a wff *W*, first you define functions on the statement letters to the set TF. Then by repeated use of the following tables you'll find a mapping of *W* to TF.

A	NOT *A*
TRUE	FALSE
FALSE	TRUE

A	*B*	*A* AND *B*
TRUE	TRUE	TRUE
TRUE	FALSE	FALSE
FALSE	TRUE	FALSE
FALSE	FALSE	FALSE

A	*B*	*A* OR *B*
TRUE	TRUE	TRUE
TRUE	FALSE	TRUE
FALSE	TRUE	TRUE
FALSE	FALSE	FALSE

Notice that the OR is non-exclusive.

Now IMPLIES can be added to AND, OR, and NOT, and is defined as follows: (*A* IMPLIES *B*) equals ((NOT *A*) OR *B*). This definition, while similar to, is not exactly the same as the way that implication is usually defined in everyday language, as will be demonstrated. From the definition given here you obtain (by substitution) the truth table:

A	*B*	*A* IMPLIES *B*
TRUE	TRUE	TRUE
TRUE	FALSE	FALSE
FALSE	TRUE	TRUE
FALSE	FALSE	TRUE

so that this IMPLIES is true when the premise is false or the conclusion is true even if the premise has no relationship whatsoever to the conclusion. In everyday language the formation of the sentence *A* IMPLIES *B* is not even contemplated when *A* has no relationship to *B*. For example, one would not form the sentence "My dog is a unicorn implies oranges are apples." However, because the premise is false this sentence is true in propositional calculus. Furthermore, because propositional calculus (with statement letters replaced by predicates) is a part of first-order logic which, in turn, forms a foundation for modern mathematics, then modern mathematics involves the type of implication defined here. This fact might seem confusing, especially in the case of statements such as "Every element of the empty set has the value two," which is true because the empty set has no elements. In other words, "x is a member of the empty set implies $x = 2$" is true in mathematics because the statement "x is a member of the empty set" is false, and a false premise implies any conclusion.

The motivation for this meaning for IMPLIES is to fit IMPLIES into a two-valued logic. Essentially it does no harm because mathematicians are not concerned about implications where the premise is false. Of course, mathematics is not confined to two-valued logic, but that is another story that we shall not go into here.

Example

Consider the wff *W*:

(((*A* IMPLIES *B*) AND (*B* IMPLIES *C*)) IMPLIES (*A* IMPLIES *C*))

If you assign TRUE to *A*, FALSE to *B* and FALSE to *C*, then, (*A* IMPLIES *B*) has the value FALSE and (*B* IMPLIES *C*) has the value TRUE. Thus, ((*A* IMPLIES *B*) AND (*B* IMPLIES *C*)) has the value FALSE. And therefore, the entire wff has the value TRUE.

Consequently, for this assignment of values to the statement letters, *W* has the value TRUE. As it turns out *W* has the value TRUE for any assignment of values to the variables. In propositional calculus a wff with this property is called a *tautology*. The tautologies of propositional calculus are exactly the theorems of propositional calculus. Thus, this interpretation of propositional calculus along with the use of truth tables turns out to be an effective means for determining whether or not a given wff is a theorem. We have left out the axioms and rules of inference for propositional calculus because they are not needed here. (For a more extensive treatment of propositional calculus see the references listed for Mendelson and Church in the Bibliography.)

Predicates and quantifiers

In symbolic logic it is necessary to be able to assert that something has a given property or that two or more things have a certain relationship. Properties and relationships are called *predicates*. For example, "Bill is John's brother" or "That is a donkey." You can write $B(b,j)$ to stand for "Bill is John's brother" where b stands for Bill, j stands for John, and $B(x,y)$ is the predicate "x is the brother of y." Here $B(\, , \,)$, b, and j are constants while x and y are variables and can have various constants substituted for them. You could also write $D(x)$ to stand for "x is a donkey" where $D(\,)$ is a constant predicate and x is a variable. B is a *two-place*, or *binary, predicate* and D is a *single-place*, or *monadic predicate*. In order to accommodate these new parts of language, we need to extend our previous definitions for wfs. In first-order logic, the letters from the beginning of the alphabet, a,b,c,. . . are used for *constants* and letters from the end of the alphabet, x,y,z for *variables*. There is an infinite list of *function letters*, f_i. Each f_i will have an integer $n_i >= 1$ associated with it; and f will, thus, be said to be "an n-place function" where $n = n_i$. Further, there is an infinite number of predicate letters P_i and each P_i will also have an integer $m_i >= 1$ associated with it where m_i is the number of arguments associated with it.

Terms are defined as follows:

1. Variables and constants are terms.
2. If f_i is an n-place function and $t_1,t_2,...,t_n$ are terms then $f(t_1,t_2,...,t_n)$ is a term.

Atomic formulas are defined to be n-place predicates with n terms filled in. For example, if P is an n-place predicate, then $P(t_1,t_2,...,t_n)$ is an atomic formula.

Examples of functions are plus and times. For example if $f(x,y)$ stands for $x + y$, then $f(3,4) = 7$.

Let $P(x)$ stand for an n-place predicate having x as a variable.

Quantifiers in this context are "for all" and "there exists." We will write "for all" as (x) where x is a variable. Then $(x)P(x)$ means "for all x the predicate P holds." We will write $E(x)$ to stand for "there exists an x such that . . ." so that $E(x)P(x)$ stands for "there exists an x such that P holds for x" or just "there exists an x such that P of x."

The well-formed formulas (wfs) are built up as follows:

1. Every atomic formula is a wff.
2. If X is a wff then (NOT X) is a wff.
3. If X and Y are wfs then (X AND Y) is a wff.
4. If X and Y are wfs then (X OR Y) is a wff.
5. If X is a wff then $((x)X)$ is a wff.
6. If X is a wff then $(E(x)X)$ is a wff.

If, in propositional calculus, you replace statement letters by predicates with terms filled in, you obtain a subset of the predicate calculus. This can be seen by noticing that rules one to four above are the same as for propositional calculus.

In $((x)X)$, where X is a wff, X is called the *scope* of (x) because (x) and X are within the same outer parentheses. In the case of (((x)X) AND Y) Y is "not within the scope of (x)." If X does not contain the variable x then $((x)X)$ is to be replaced by X.

$E(x)$ could be dispensed with because $(E(x)X)$ is taken to be the same as (NOT ((x) (NOT X))). However, we shall keep $E(x)$ because it makes some expressions briefer.

Free and bound variables

It is important to distinguish between free and bound variables because the two types are interpreted differently. Therefore, you have the following technical definition.

An occurrence of a variable x in a wff X is said to be *bound* in X if (x) (or $E(x)$) occurs in X and the occurrence of x is within the scope of (x) (or $E(x)$). Also an occurrence of x (x) or (x) is said to be bound. If an occurrence of a variable x in X is not within the scope of a quantifier (x) or $E(x)$, then that occurrence of x is said to be *free* in X.

Example

In $A(x_1,x_2)$ OR $(x_1)B(x_1)$ the occurrence of x_1 in A is free and the occurrence of x_1 in B is bound. The occurrence of x_1 in (x_1) is also bound.

We modify rules five and six above for wfs by allowing $((x)X)$ and $(E(x)X)$ only when x has a free occurrence in X.

Interpretations for predicate calculus

The development in this section is based on the *Logic, Semantics, Metamathematics* papers by A. Tarski. (See also the sources listed in the Bibliography for the Mendelson and Church entries.)

In first-order logic an interpretation consists of:

1. A non-empty set S called the domain of the interpretation.
2. An assignment to each n-place predicate of an n-place relation on S. A relation on S is a set of n-tuples of S. For example, if S is the set of integers, then the relation "greater than" is the set of all ordered pairs (i,j) such that i is greater than j.
3. An assignment to each n-place function of an n-place function on S into S.
4. An assignment to each constant letter of an element of S.

Given a wff W having n variables $x_1,x_2,..,x_n$ and a sequence SEQ $b_1,b_2,...,b_n$ of n members of S (possibly with repeats), check whether or not "SEQ satisfies W" as follows:

1. Wherever x_i occurs in W, substitute b_i for it.
2. Wherever a constant occurs in W, substitute the corresponding member of S given by definition four in the previous list.
3. For each function in W, perform the corresponding function on S, given by definition three in the previous list, and replace the function by the resulting element of S.
4. For each predicate P in W, check to see that the tuple of members of S in P is a tuple in the relation given by definition two in the previous list. If so, replace P by SATISFIED, otherwise replace P by NOT SATISFIED.
5. Replace (NOT (SATISFIED)) by (NOT SATISFIED) and replace (NOT (NOT SATISFIED)) by (SATISFIED).
6. Replace:

    ((SATISFIED) AND (SATISFIED)) by (SATISFIED),
    ((SATISFIED) AND (NOT SATISFIED)) by (NOT SATISFIED),
    ((NOT SATISFIED) AND (SATISFIED)) by (NOT SATISFIED),
    and
    ((NOT SATISFIED) AND (NOT SATISFIED)) by (NOT SATISFIED).
7. Replace:

    ((SATISFIED) OR (SATISFIED)) by (SATISFIED),
    ((SATISFIED) OR (NOT SATISFIED)) by (SATISFIED),
    ((NOT SATISFIED) OR (SATISFIED)) by (SATISFIED), and
    ((NOT SATISFIED) OR (NOT SATISFIED)) by (NOT SATISFIED).
8. Replace $(x_i)X$ by SATISFIED if every sequence of n elements from S, which differs from SEQ in at most the i'th element results in X being replaced by SATISFIED. Otherwise, replace $(x_i)X$ by NOT SATISFIED.

9. Replace $E(x_i)X$ by SATISFIED if there exists a sequence of n elements from S, which differs from SEQ in at most the i'th element such that it results in X being replaced by SATISFIED. Otherwise, replace $E(x_i)X$ by NOT SATISFIED.

By repeated use of these nine steps, the wff W will eventually be replaced either by SATISFIED or NOT SATISFIED. If W is replaced by SATISFIED, we say "SEQ satisfies W."

If W is a wff with n variables and I is an interpretation of W with domain S, then W is said to be "true with respect to I" if W is satisfied by every n element sequence from S. W is said to be "false with respect to I" if W is not satisfied by any n element sequence from S.

If G is a set of wfs and I is an interpretation for all the wfs in G, such that each wff in G is true with respect to I, then, I is said to be a "model for G." The theory of models plays an important role in modern mathematics. (See the resources listed in the Cohn entry in the Bibliography for further information.)

In the last 25 years a new approach to the foundations of mathematics, logic, interpretations, and models, has developed in a subject area of mathematics called *category theory*. This development promises to have great significance for query languages and computer science. (Category theory is beyond the scope of this book. For more information consult the article by Makkai and Reyes and the book by Barr and Wells, referenced in the Bibliography.)

Recently, more and more logical systems are being used in computer science. This development is called logic programming. The 1984 article by Goguen and Burstall—*Introducing Institutions, Lecture Notes*—is a good starting point for anyone who would like to know more about logic programming.

Tuple relational calculus

In his 1971 article Codd, having in mind a query language for relational databases using concepts of first-order logic, developed what he called relational calculus. Given a database scheme D he limited his predicates, terms, and wfs based on D. Then, he defined an interpretation of the resulting calculus in such a way that each wff corresponded to a query whose result is those tuples that satisfy the wff. We shall do what Codd did but in a slightly different way to maintain a greater similarity to the development of first-order logic.

In the following we assume a universe of attributes $U = \{A_1,A_2,...,A_k\}$, and a database scheme $D = \{R_1,R_2,...,R_l\}$, where each R_i is a relation scheme over some subset of the attributes in U. Furthermore, we assume a finite relation r_i over each relation scheme R_i.

Given D we start with an interpretation whose set S of elements is the union of the relations over the relation schemes in D. There will be an infinite set of variables x_i, $i >= 1$ and an infinite set of constants $a_i, i >= 1$. For each attribute A_i *in* U let f_i be a function letter. There will be l unary predicates $P_1, P_2, \ldots, P_l$. The meaning of $P_i(x)$ is "x is a tuple in r_i." In other words, in our interpretation $P_i(x)$ is satisfied if and only if x is a tuple in r_i. There will be five binary predicates $P=$, $P>$, $P<$, $P<=$, and $P>=$.

Terms will be either variables or $f(x)$ where x is a variable and f is a function. If P is a unary predicate and x is a variable then $P(x)$ is an atomic formula. If P is one of the binary predicates, f_i and f_j are function letters, and x and y are variables, and the domains of A_i and A_j are comparable, then $P(f_i(x), f_j(y))$ is an atomic formula. Similarly, $P(f_i(x), a)$ is an atomic formula where a is constrained to be interpreted into values which are comparable to those in the domain of A_i.

The meaning of $P_C(f_i(x), f_j(y))$ is "$f_i(x) C f_j(y)$" where C is one of the comparators $=$, $>$, $<$, $<=$, $>=$. In other words, if, in our interpretation, x is mapped into a tuple u and y is mapped into a tuple v such that the value of u at attribute i is in the relationship C to the value of v at j, then $P_C(f_i(x), f_j(y))$ is satisfied and otherwise $P_C(f_i(x), f_j(y))$ is not satisfied. Similarly the meaning of $P_C(f_i(x), a)$ is "$f_i(x)\ C\ a$" where the obvious rule holds for satisfied and not satisfied.

Given these atomic formulas, we define simple wfs as follows:

1. Every simple wff must be of the form

   U_1 AND U_2 AND...AND U_n AND V

   where each U_i is $P(x)$ for some unary predicate P and every free variable in V appears in one of the U_i.

   Thus, in our interpretation, if x is a free variable then x must appear in P_i for some i and thus x must be mapped into a member of S which is also a member of r_i. In other words, the U_i merely tell us what tables the tuple variables belong to.

   Furthermore, if x is a variable which appears in P_i then $f_j(x)$ is allowed only if A_j is a member of R_i. (We say j is "acceptable for x.")

   Then, if x is mapped into the tuple t in r_i, $f_j(t) = t(A_j)$.

   If a is a constant variable then a will be mapped into a member of the domain of some attribute in U. If two terms occur in a binary predicate then they must be comparable. For example, strings are not to be compared with numbers. Similarly, if a term and a constant letter a occur in a binary predicate, they must be comparable.

2. If x is a bound variable appearing in V within the scope of a quantifier $Q(x)$ then there must be a unary predicate P such that $P(x)$ appears within the scope of Q, but NOT $P(x)$ does not appear within the scope of Q and no other unary predicate P' with x in it occurs within the scope of Q. This rule is clearly necessary to determine

the interpretation of x, namely those tuples that x can be mapped into, or, to put it another way, which table in the database the variable x refers to.

Simple alpha expressions

Following Codd we define a *simple alpha expression* as an expression of the form:

$$(t_1,t_2,\ldots,t_k) : w$$

where:

1. w is a simple wff.
2. $t_1,t_2,\ldots,t_k$ are distinct terms each being a free variable in w or being $f_i(x)$ where x is a free variable in w, and i is acceptable for x. Codd calls this list of terms the *target list*.
3. The set of variables occurring in $t_1,t_2,\ldots,t_k$ corresponds exactly to the set of free variables in w. The list $(t_1,t_2,\ldots,t_k)$ is called the *target list*, and w is called the *qualification expression*.

Alpha expressions

Following Codd we generalize the notion of simple alpha expressions to alpha expressions as follows:

1. Every simple alpha expression is an alpha expression.
2. If $t{:}w_1$ and $t{:}w_2$ are alpha expressions then

   t: (w_1 OR w_2),
   t: (w_1 AND (NOT w_2)),

   and

   t: (w_1 AND w_2)

   are alpha expressions.

Example

Let D be a database scheme over the set of attributes U = {flight_number, type_of_plane,gate_number}, with relation schemes:

Type = {flight_number,type_of_plane}, and Gate = {flight_number, gate_number}.

Let the relations for Type and Gate be as follows:

Type:	flight_number	type_of_plane
	101	747
	205	737
	315	747

Gate:	flight_number	gate_number
	101	10
	205	15
	315	20

For our interpretation, our set S is simply {<101,747>,<205,737>, <315,747>,<101,10>,<205,15>,<315,20>}. We have three function letters which we will denote by the names of the attributes in U, and two unary predicates which we will call Type and Gate. Thus, Type(x) will mean that x is a variable that may be mapped to a tuple in the relation Type, and Gate(x) will mean that x is a variable that can be mapped to a tuple in the relation Gate.

Consider the simple alpha expression:

type_of_plane(x) : Type(x) AND E(y) ((Gate(y) AND (flight number(x) = flight_number(y)) AND (gate_number(y) = a)))

It is easy to see that this expression corresponds to the set of queries: "Find the types of planes whose flights have gate number a." This is a set of queries rather than just one query because the interpretation of a has not been determined. As soon as you decide on the interpretation of the constant a you have a query. For example, if the interpretation of a is 10, then the answer to the query is {<747>}. (Place {} around 747 because the answer to a query is always a set of tuples—in this case a one-member set of tuples.)

Once the constants in an alpha expression have been interpreted, the answer to a query is carried out by means of a generalization of the idea of satisfiability for the first-order logic. In the case of our query above, with a mapped to 10, we consider all pairs of tuples, t_1 and t_2, from the set S such that t_1 is a member of Type and t_2 is a member of Gate. We map x to t_1 and y to t_2. Having done that, Type(x) is satisfied by t_1 and Gate(y) is satisfied by t_2, and (gate_number(y) = 10) is satisfied only when t_2 = <101,10>, thus limiting us to pairs of tuples t_1 and t_2 where t_2 = <101,10>. Because there is only one tuple in Gate where flight_number = 101, namely t_1 = <101,747>, the only pair of tuples satisfying (flight_number(x) = flight_number(y)) AND (gate_number(y) = 10) is <101,747> and <101,10>.

Finally, we select the members of <101,747> and <101,10> that are in the target list, in this case {<747>}. It is easy to check that the formulation of our alpha expressions depends only on the database scheme, and not on the relations that constitute an *instance* of the database scheme. Once the interpretation of the constants in the alpha expressions has been determined, the result of the query depends on the relations of the database scheme.

Codd defined a query language L to be relationally complete only if every query formulated by alpha expressions could be formulated in *L*. Date outlines a proof that SQL is relationally complete.

Converting alpha expressions to SQL expressions

Given the query:

type_of_plane(*x*) : Type(*x*) AND E(*y*)((Gate(*y*) AND (flight number(*x*) = flight_number(*y*)) AND (gate_number(*y*) = 10)))

you can convert it to a SQL query as follows:

```
SELECT    type_of_plane
FROM      Type
WHERE     flight_number IN
(SELECT   flight_number
FROM      Gate
WHERE     gate_number = 10);
```

Example

The following example illustrates the use of IMPLIES and a quantifier, (*y*) and their translation to SQL.

type_of_plane(*x*) : Type(*x*) AND (*y*)(((Gate(*y*) AND (flight number(*x*) = flight_number(*y*)) AND (gate_number(*y*) = 10))) IMPLIES (type_of_plane(*x*) = 747))

Recall that *A* IMPLIES *B* is shorthand for NOT *A* OR *B*. Consider the tuple <205,737> from Type. By rule eight in the earlier section of this chapter entitled "Interpretations for predicate calculus," this tuple satisfies the qualification clause *v* if and only if every tuple *t* in Gate satisfies *W* = ((205 = flight_number(*t*)) AND (gate_number(*t*) = 10)) IMPLIES (737 = 747). Because no tuple in Gate SATISFIES ((205 = flight_number(*t*)) AND (gate_number(*t*)) = 10)), every tuple in Gate satisfies *W*. Thus <205,737> satisfies the qualification clause of our query.

Furthermore, every tuple in Type satisfies our query. Thus, the result of our query is the list <747>, <737>.

Our query:

type_of_plane(*x*) : Type(*x*) AND (*y*)(((Gate(*y*) AND (flight number(*x*) = flight_number(*y*)) AND (gate_number(*y*) = 10))) IMPLIES (type_of_plane(*x*) = 747))

translates into SQL as:

```
SELECT    type_of_plane
FROM      Type
```

```
WHERE    flight_number not IN
(SELECT  flight_number
FROM     Gate
WHERE    gate_number = 10)
OR       flight_number IN
(SELECT  flight_number
FROM     Gate
WHERE    (gate_number = 10) AND (type_of_plane = 747));
```

Other examples of translating tuple relational calculus expressions into SQL queries are given in the exercises at the end of this chapter.

Chapter 15 exercises

15.1 Express OR in terms of NOT and AND and show that the resulting expression has the same truth table as OR.

15.2 Find an expression for exclusive OR in terms of NOT, AND, and OR; and compute the truth table to see that you have the correct expression.

15.3 Show that *A* IMPLIES *A* is a tautology.

15.4a Consider the following addition table for the integers mod(5). (Do ordinary addition. If the result is >= 5 repeatedly subtract 5 until the result is < 5.)

+	**0**	**1**	**2**	**3**	**4**
0	0	1	2	3	4
1	1	2	3	4	0
2	2	3	4	0	1
3	3	4	0	1	2
4	4	0	1	2	3

Make this into a model for the expression:
$E = (x)((y)(E(z)\ (P(f(y,z),\ x))))$.

15.4b Do the same for multiplication mod(5) and the expression: F = $(x)((y)((\text{NOT } P(y,a)) \text{ IMPLIES } E(z)(P(f(y,z),x))))$.

15.4c Can you make multiplication mod(4) into a model for *E*?

15.5 Let *T* be the table below with attributes *A*, *B*, *C* such that, in a given row, the value in column *A* times the value in column *B* equals mod(3) the value in column *C*. Formulate a simple alpha expression to find the solution of the equation 2 times $x = 1$. Translate the alpha expression into a SQL SELECT query.

	T	
A	*B*	*C*
0	0	0
0	1	0
0	2	0
1	0	0
1	1	1
1	2	2
2	0	0
2	1	2
2	2	1

15.6 Consider the jail database with attribute set:

u = {booking_number, prisoner_name,
prisoner_alias,
prisoner_id_number,
date_of_birth,
date_of_arrest,
charge}.

Let the relation schemes for the jail database be:

ID = {booking_number,prisoner_name,prisoner_id_number},
ALIAS = {prisoner_id_number,prisoner_alias},
BIRTH = {prisoner_id_number,date_of_birth},
ARREST = {booking_number,date_of_arrest,charge}.

Consequently, the database scheme is {ID,ALIAS,BIRTH,ARREST}. For each of the following queries find an alpha expression and the corresponding SQL SELECT statement.

15.6a Find the names of all prisoners arrested on May 6.

15.6b Find all aliases of prisoners arrested May 6.

15.6c Find all the charges against the prisoner Donald Duck.

15.6d Find the names of all prisoners who were born on Sept 8, 1960.

15.6e Find the names of all prisoners arrested May 6 charged with DUI.

Answers to chapter 15 exercises

15.1 NOT((NOT *A*) AND (NOT *B*)). Compute the truth table in stages as follows:

```
NOT((NOT A   )  AND   (NOT B   ))
        TRUE               TRUE
        FALSE              FALSE
                  FALSE
              TRUE
NOT((NOT A   )  AND   (NOT B   ))
        TRUE               FALSE
        FALSE              TRUE
                  FALSE
              TRUE
NOT((NOT A   )  AND   (NOT B   ))
        FALSE              TRUE
        TRUE               FALSE
                  FALSE
              TRUE
NOT((NOT A   )  AND   (NOT B   ))
        FALSE              FALSE
        TRUE               TRUE
                  TRUE
              FALSE
```

15.2 (*A* OR *B*) AND (NOT(*A* AND *B*)). For *A* TRUE and *B* TRUE you have:

```
(A     OR B   )   AND   (NOT (A    AND    B  ))
TRUE   TRUE                  TRUE         TRUE
   TRUE                             TRUE
                                FALSE
                     FALSE
```

Check the other rows of the truth table similarly.

15.3 For *A* TRUE:

```
   A      IMPLIES     A
 TRUE      TRUE
                    TRUE
```

For *A* FALSE:

```
   A      IMPLIES     A
 FALSE     FALSE
                    TRUE
```

Because the bottom line is TRUE in both of the possible cases this is a tautology.

15.4a Let *f* be mapped into addition as in the table. Let *P* be mapped into equality. Let S be the set {0,1,2,3,4}. Let SEQ be all two-element sequences of elements from S. For all members, {*a*,*b*}, of SEQ find a member *c* of S such that $b + c = a$. For example, {1,4} is a member of SEQ and you have 4 + 2 = 1. Because it is possible to do this for every pair in SEQ, S, with the addition in the table, is a model for *E*.

15.4b In the case of multiplication mod(5) the table is:

x	**0**	**1**	**2**	**3**	**4**
0	0	0	0	0	0
1	0	1	2	3	4
2	0	2	4	1	3
3	0	3	1	4	2
4	0	4	3	2	1

Map *a* into 0, *f* into multiplication, and proceed as in the case of addition.

15.4c No. The table is:

x	**0**	**1**	**2**	**3**
0	0	0	0	0
1	0	1	2	3
2	0	2	0	2
3	0	3	2	1

and for the pair {1,2} there is no a such that $a \times 2 = 1$.

15.5 The alpha expression is:

$t[B] : P_T(t)$ AND $((t[A] = 2)$ AND $(t[C] = 1))$

The corresponding SQL expression is:

```
SELECT   B
FROM     T
WHERE    A = 2 AND C = 1;
```

15.6a *t*[prisoner_name] :
ID(*t*)
AND *E*(*u*)(ARREST(*u*)
AND (*u*(date_of_arrest) = May 6)
AND (*u*(booking_number) = *t*(booking_number)).

The corresponding SQL expression is:

```
SELECT prisoner_name
FROM ID
WHERE booking_number IN
```

```
(SELECT booking_number
FROM ARREST
WHERE date_of_arrest = 'May 6' );
```

15.6b t[prisoner_alias] :
ALIAS(t)
AND E(u)(ARREST(u)
AND (u(date_of_arrest) = May 6)
AND E(v)(ID(v)
AND (v(booking_number) = u(booking_number)
AND (v(prisoner_id_number) = t(prisoner_id_number)))))

The corresponding SQL expression is:

```
SELECT prisoner_alias
FROM ALIAS
WHERE prisoner_id_number IN
(SELECT prisoner_id_number
FROM ID
WHERE booking_number IN
(SELECT booking_number
FROM ARREST
WHERE date_of_arrest = 'May 6' ));
```

15.6c t[charge] :
ARREST(t)
AND E(u)(ID(u)
AND (u(booking_number) = t(booking_number))
AND (u(prisoner_name) = Donald Duck))

The corresponding SQL expression is:

```
SELECT charge
FROM ARREST
WHERE booking_number IN
(SELECT booking_number
FROM ID
WHERE prisoner_name = 'Donald Duck');
```

15.6d t[prisoner_name] :
ID(t)
AND E(u)(BIRTH(u)
AND (t(prisoner_id_number) = u(prisoner_id_number))
AND (u(date_of_birth) = 'Sept 8 1960'))

The corresponding SQL expression is:

```
SELECT prisoner_name
FROM ID
```

```
WHERE prisoner_id_number IN
(SELECT prisoner_id_number
FROM BIRTH
WHERE date_of_birth = 'Sept 8 1960');
```

15.6e t[prisoner_name]:
ID(t)
AND E(u)(ARREST(u)
AND (t(booking_number) = u(booking_number))
AND (u(date_of_arrest) = May 6)
AND (u(charge) = DUI))

The corresponding SQL expression is:

```
SELECT prisoner_name
FROM ID
WHERE booking_number IN
(SELECT booking_number
FROM ARREST
WHERE date_of_arrest = 'May 6' AND charge = 'DUI');
```

Glossary

aggregate function This is a group function. A function operating on the values in one column of a table and producing a single value as its result.

alpha expression E.F. Codd's term for a query in tuple relational calculus.

argument An expression inside the parentheses of a function, supplying a value on which the function will operate.

ASCII A standard for using digital data to represent printable characters. An acronym for *American Standard Code for Information Exchange*.

atomic formula An *n*-place predicate with *n* terms to be entered.

attribute A column heading in a table.

base table Any "real" table in the database, as opposed to a virtual table.

Boolean operators In relational algebra, Union (the set of all tuples that are in either one of two relations), Intersect (the set of all tuples that are in both of two relations) and Difference (the set of all tuples that are in one but not the other).

bound variable An occurrence of a variable x in a wff where (x) or $E\ (x)$ occurs in X and the occurrence of x is within the scope of $(x\ )$ or $E\ (x\ )$. Contrast with *free variable*.

C language A programming language.

candidate row A row selected by a main query, the field values of which are used in the execution of a correlated subquery.

Cartesian product An equijoin where the set of conditions is empty.

category theory A relatively new subject area of mathematics, developed in recent years as an approach to the foundations of mathematics, logic, interpretations, and models.

CHAR A datatype that stores character strings.

character string A sequence of characters.

COMMIT Make permanent changes to the database. Before inserts, updates, deletes are stored, both old and new data exist so changes can be stored or data can be restored to its previous state. When data are committed, all new data that is part of the transaction are made permanent, thereby replacing the old data in the database.

concatenated index An index created on more than one column of a table. Used to guarantee that those columns are unique for every row in the table.

database administrator (DBA) A user authorized to grant and revoke other users' access to the system, modify options affecting all users, and perform other administrative functions.

database objects Individual databases in a database management system, as well as the tables, views, indices, synonyms, aliases, columns, and rows that are created.

Data Control Language (DCL) One category of SQL statements. These statements control access to the data and to the database. Examples: GRANT CONNECT, GRANT SELECT, and REVOKE DBA.

Data Definition Language (DDL) One category of SQL statements. These statements define (CREATE) or delete (DROP) database objects. Examples: CREATE VIEW, CREATE TABLE, CREATE INDEX, and DROP TABLE.

data dictionary A comprehensive set of tables and views usually owned by the DBA. Also contains information available to the DBA only about users, privileges, and auditing. A central source of information for the database itself and for all users.

Data Manipulation Language (DML) One category of SQL statements. These statements query and update the actual data. Examples: SELECT, INSERT, DELETE, and UPDATE.

datatype Any one of the forms of data stored and manipulated. The major datatypes are: CHAR, DATE, LONG, NUMBER, and RAW.

date field A field whose value is a date. Sometimes applied to a field whose value is a number representing a date.

datum A single unit of data.

DBA *See* database administrator.

deadlock A situation where two users are each vying for resources locked by the other, and therefore neither user can obtain the necessary resource to complete the work.

default The value of any option that is built into the system and that will be used by the system if the user fails to specify a value for that option.

distinct Unique.

domain relational calculus One of the two forms of relational calculus in recent literature. (The other form is *tuple relational calculus.*) In domain relational calculus, the variables refer to attributes instead of rows.

dummy table A table containing exactly one row. Useful as the object of a SELECT command intended to copy the value of one field to another field.

embedded SQL An application program consisting of programming language text and SQL text.

equijoin A join condition specifying the relationship equals (=).

export To transfer database files into some other storage area.

expression One or more data items combined with operators or functions in a command.

field A part of a table that holds one piece of data. The intersection of a row and a column.

filetype The part of a file's name that describes the type of data stored in the file. Usually, a file's filetype is separated from the file name by a period, like this: STORDATA.LIS, where LIS is the filetype.

foreign key A column (or combination of columns) in a table where it is not a key in that table, but is a key in another table. Used for relating data in multiple tables using joins.

formfeed A control character that causes the printer to skip to the top of a new sheet of paper.

free variable An occurrence of a variable x in X not within the scope of a quantifier (x) or $E\ (x)$. Contrast with *bound variable*.

function An operation that may be performed by placing the function's name in an expression. Most functions take one or more arguments within the parentheses, and use the value(s) of the argument(s) in the operation.

group function A function operating on a column or expression in all of the rows selected by a query, and computing a single value from them. Example: AVG, which computes an average. Same as aggregate function or built-in function.

hexadecimal notation A numbering system using base 16 instead of base 10. It represents the numbers 10 through 15 by the letters A through F. Often used to represent the internal (raw) values of data stored in a computer.

index A feature used primarily to speed execution and impose uniqueness on data. Provides faster access to data than doing a full table scan.

initialization The initial preparing of a database. Always done when installing a database system for the first time.

join Retrieval from more than one table.

Julian date A means of converting date data so every date can be expressed as a unique integer, thus allowing arithmetic operations to be performed on the data.

key The column(s) in one table that can be used to uniquely identify a row. Column(s) forming a key are usually indexed.

main query The outermost query in a query containing a subquery. The query that displays a result.

main variable A variable that receives a field value in an EXEC SQL command.

modus ponens A rule of inference whereby some wfs can be derived from others.

natural join An equijoin taken on the common column of two tables with the duplicate of the common column removed.

nested SELECT *See* subquery.

nesting An arrangement of two processing steps in which one invokes the other.

non-equijoin A join condition specifying a relationship other than equals, for example <, >, < =, > =.

null Empty. Not a value, but the absence of a value.

Null Value Function Used in the ORACLE RDBMS version of SQL to convert a null value to a specified non-null value, for example zero, for the purpose of evaluating an expression or function.

NUMBER datatype A datatype for numeric data.

object Something stored in a database. Examples: tables, views, synonyms, indexes, columns, reports, stored procedures, and stored programs.

outer join Rows that match one, but not both of the join conditions.

parameter A column name, expression or constant specifying what a command should do.

portability The ease with which a computer program can be adapted to hardware different from that for which it was written.

precedence The order in which the RDBMS performs operations on an expression.

pre-compiler A program that reads a source program file and writes a modified source program file that a compiler can then read.

predicate clause A clause based on one of the operators (=, !=, IS, IS NOT, >, >=, <, <=) and containing no AND, OR or NOT.

propagation The process of copying a value from one field to another logically related field, or computing a value to be stored in a related field. For example: when an employee's Social Security Number is entered in a block of a salary record form, it may be propagated to a block of a withholding tax form.

proof A sequence of wfs such that each is either an axiom or can be derived from those preceding it by one of the rules of inference.

public synonym A synonym for a database object that the DBA has created for use by all users.

query An instruction to SQL that will retrieve information from one or more tables or views.

RAW datatype Similar to CHAR datatype, except that it stores uninterpreted bytes rather than characters.

read consistency Feature whereby a SQL query always sees a snapshot of a table as it existed at the start of query execution even when others are modifying the table.

record One row of a table.

recursive definition A definition where the rule may be repeated an arbitrary number of times.

relational algebra A set of operations on relations each of which produces other relations.

relational calculus A development by E.F. Codd of the first-order logic for constructing queries on relational databases. It consists of tuple relational calculus and domain relational calculus.

relational database A database that appears to the user to be just a collection of tables.

reserved word A word with a special meaning in SQL and therefore not available to users in naming tables, views or columns.

result table A temporary table formed by SQL as a result of your query.

rollback To undo changes made to the database during a transaction or logical unit of work by using the ROLLBACK command. Opposite of the COMMIT command.

schema In the theory of relational databases, a synonym for *set*. A *database schema* is a set of tables in the database. For a table, the list of columns is a schema.

split-screen scrolling A feature of some display devices making it possible to scroll data in a range of lines without affecting other parts of the screen.

SQL *See* Structured Query Language.

Structured Query Language (SQL) A basic user interface for storing and retrieving information in the database.

subquery A query used as a clause in a SQL command.

substitution variable A variable name or numeral used in a command file to represent a value that will be provided when the command file is run.

syntax The linear order of words or symbols.

TPS (Transaction Processing Subsystem) An ORACLE facility first available with version 6. A high-performance, fault-tolerant system designed for online transaction processing and large database applications. Its two main features are (1) the row-level lock manager, and (2) PL/SQL, a new programming language that allows you to combine SQL with a procedural language.

temporary tables Frequently required to order data and to execute SQL statements including DISTINCT, ORDER BY, and GROUP BY clauses.

transaction A logical unit of work as defined by the user.

transaction processing The processing of logical units of work, rather than individual entries, to keep the database consistent.

Transaction Processing Subsystem *See* TPS.

truth function A set of mappings from wfs to the set TF = (TRUE, FALSE). The main interpretation for propositional calculus.

tuple Row.

tuple relational calculus One of the two types of the relational calculus. (The other is *domain relational calculus*.) In tuple relational calculus, the variables refer to tuples or rows in relations.

unique index An index that imposes uniqueness on each value it indexes. May be a single column or concatenated columns.

union The union operator of traditional set theory, for example A UNION *B* (where *A* and *B* are sets) is the set of all objects *x* such that *x* is a member of *A* or *x* is a member of *B*, or both).

unit of work A logical unit of work is equivalent to a transaction. Includes all SQL statements since you either logged on, last committed or last rolled back your work. A transaction can encompass one SQL statement or many SQL statements.

view A table that does not physically exist as such in storage, but looks to the user as though it does. A part of a table that does exist in the database. Also known as a *virtual table*.

virtual column A column in a query result the value of which was calculated from the value(s) of other column(s).

virtual table A table that does not actually exist in the database, but looks to the user as though it does. Contrast with *base table*. *See* view.

wff A single well-formed formula.

wfs More than one well-formed formula.

wrapping Moving the end of a heading or field to a new line when it is too long to fit on one line.

Bibliography

American National Standard For Information Systems. Database Language—SQL. ANSI X3.135-1986. American National Standards Institute, Inc. 1430 Broadway, NY, NY 10018.

_______. Database Language—SQL with Integrity Enhancement. ANSI X3.135-1989. American National Standards Institute, Inc. 1430 Broadway, NY, NY 10018.

_______. Database Language—Embedded SQL. ANSI X3.168-1989. American National Standards Institute, Inc. 1430 Broadway, NY, NY 10018.

Astrahan, M. M., and Chamberlin, D. D. Implementation of a structured English query language. *Communications of the ACM*, vol. 18, no. 10 (October 1975): 580–588.

Astrahan, M. M., Blasgen, M. W., Chamberlin, D. D., Eswaran, K. P., Gray, J. N., Griffiths, P. P., King, W. F., Lorie, R. A., McJones, P. R., Mehl, J. W., Putzolu, G. R., Traiger, I. L., Wade, B., and Watson, V. System R: A relational approach to database management. *ACM Transactions on Database Systems* (June 1976): 97.

Bancilhov, F. and Spyratos, N. Update semantics of relational views. *ACM Transactions on Database Systems*, vol. 6, no. 4 (December 1981): 557–575.

Barr, M. and Wells, C. *Toposes, Triples, and Theories* NY: Springer-Verlag, 1985.

Boyce, R. F. and Chamberlin, D. D. Using a structured English query language as a data definition facility. *IBM Research Report RJ 1318 (#20559)* December 10, 1973.

Boyce, R. F. Chamberlin, D. D., King, W. F., and Hammer, M. M. Specifying queries as relational expressions: The SQUARE data sublanguage. *Communications of the ACM*, vol. 18, no. 11 (Nov. 1975): 621–628.

Celko, Joe. Cracks in the ANSI Wall. *Database Programming & Design*, vol. 2, no. 6 (June 1989).

———. Celko on SQL. *Database Programming & Design*, vol. 3, no. 9 (September 1990).

Chamberlin, D. D. and Boyce, R. F. SEQUEL: A structured English query language. Proc. ACM-SIGMOD Workshop on Data Description, Access, and Control, Ann Arbor, Michigan, May 1974: 249–264.

Chamberlin, D. D., Gray, J. N, and Traiger, I. L. Views, authorization, and locking in a relational database system. Proc. 1975 National Computer Conference, Anaheim, CA: 425–430.

Chamberlin, D. D., Astrahan, M. M., Eswaran, K. P., Griffiths, P. P., Lorie, R. A., Mehl, J. W., Reisner, P. and Wade, B. W. SEQUEL 2: A unified approach to data definition, manipulation, and control. *IBM J. Res. and Develop.*, vol. 20, no. 6 (Nov. 1976): 560–575. (See also errata in January 1977 issue.)

Chamberlin, D. D. A summary of user experience with the SQL data sublanguage. Proc. Internat. Conf. Data on Bases, Aberdeen, Scotland, July 1980: 181–3. (See also *IBM Res. Rep RJ2767*, San Jose, CA, April 1980.)

Chamberlin, Donald D., Astrahan, Morton M., Blasgen, Michael W., Gray, James N., King, W. Frank, Lindsay, Bruce G., Lorie, Raymond, Mehl, James W., Price, Thomas G., Putzolu, Franco, Selinger, Patricia Griffiths, Schkolnick, Mario, Slutz, Donald R., Traiger, Irving L., Wade, Bradford W., Yost, Robert A. A history and evaluation of System R. *Communications of the ACM*, vol. 24, no. 10 (October 1981).

Church, Alonzo. *Introduction to Mathematical Logic*. Princeton, NJ: Princeton University Press, 1956.

Codd, E. F. A relational model of data for large shared data banks. *Communications of the ACM*, vol. 13, no. 6 (June 1970): 377–387.

———. Normalized data base structure: A brief tutorial. Proceedings of the 1971 SIGFIDET Workshop, Data Description Access and Control. Eds. E. F. Codd and A. L. Dean.

———. A data base sublanguge founded on the relational calculus. Proceedings of the 1971 ACM SIGFIDET Workshop, Data Description, Access and Control. Edited by E. F. Codd and A. L. Dean.

———. Relational completeness of data base sublanguages. *Data Base Systems*.

Courant Computer Science Symposia Series, vol. 6. Englewood Cliffs, NJ: Prentice-Hall, 1971.

_______. Further normalization of the data base relational model. In *Data Base Systems*. Courant Computer Science Symposia Series, vol. 6: 33–64. Englewood Cliffs, NJ: Prentice-Hall, 1971.

_______. Is Your DBMS really relational? *Computerworld* (October 14, 1985).

_______. Does your DBMS run by the rules? *Computerworld* (October 21, 1985).

_______. Extending the relational model to capture more meaning. *ACM Transactions on Database Systems* (December 1979): 397–434.

_______. *The Relational Model for Database Management: Version 2*. Reading, Massachusetts: Addison-Wesley, 1990.

Cohn, P. M. Relational structures and models. *Universal Algebra*. NY: Harper & Row, 1965.

Cosmadakis, S. and Papadimitriou, C. H. Updates of relational views. Proc. 2nd ACM SIGACT-AIGMOD Symposium on Principles of Database Systems, March 1983.

Dahl, Veronica. On database systems development through logic. *ACM Transactions on Database Systems*, vol. 7, no. 1 (March 1982).

Date, C. J. *A Guide to DB2*. Menlo Park, CA: Addison Wesley, 1985.

_______. An Introduction to Database Systems. 4th ed. Vol. 1. Menlo Park, CA: Addison Wesley, 1986.

_______. *Relational Database: Selected Writings*. Menlo Park, CA: Addison-Wesley, 1986.

_______. An architecture for high-level language database extensions. Proc. ACM SIGMOD Conference, June 1976: 101.

Dayal, U. and Bernstein, P. A. On the correct translation of update operations on relational views. *ACM TODS*, vol. 7, no. 3 (September 1982).

Fagin, R., Ullman, J. D. and Vardi, M. Y. On the semantics of updates in databases. Proc. 2nd ACM SIGACT-SIGMOD Symposium on Principles of Database Systems, March 1983.

Finkelstein, Richard. How to choose a SQL database management system. *Data Based Advisor*, vol. 5, no. 4 (April 1987).

Furtado, A. L. and Casanova, M. A. Updating relational views. *Query Processing in Database Systems*. Eds. W. Kim, D. Reiner, and D. Batory. NY: Springer-Verlag, 1985.

Goguen, J. A. and Burstall, R. M. Introducing institutions, Lecture Notes. In Logics of Programs Workshop. Carnegie Mellon University, Pittsburgh, PA. *Computer Science* 164 (June 6–8, 1983). Springer-Verlag, Berlin. 1984.

Hursch, C. J. and Hursch, J. L. SQL, the Structured Query Language, 2d Ed. Blue Ridge Summit, PA: Windcrest Books, 1991.

Hursch, J. L. The Ties that Bind. *Database Programming & Design*, vol. 2, no. 6 (June 1989).

________. Joins: More Than Meets the Eye. *Database Programming & Design*, vol. 2, no. 12 (December 1989).

________. Methods of Normalization. *Database Programming & Design*, vol. 1, no. 9 (September 1988).

Hursch, J. L. and Hursch, C. J. *Working With ORACLE: An Introduction to Database Management*. Blue Ridge Summit, PA: TAB Books, 1987.

________. *Working with ORACLE Version 6*. Blue Ridge Summit, PA: Windcrest Books, 1989.

________. *dBASE IV SQL User's Guide* Torrance, CA: Ashton-Tate, 1989.

IBM DATABASE 2 Introduction to SQL. GC26-4082, 1986. SC26-4082-2.

IBM DATABASE 2 Data Base Planning and Administration Guide. SC26-4077.

IBM DATABASE 2 Sample Application Guide, SC26-4086.

Keller, A. M. Updates to relational databases through views involving joins. *Improving Database Usability and Responsiveness* Ed. P. Scheuermann. NY: Academic Press 1982.

Kernighan, B. W. and Pike, R. *The Unix Programming Environment*. Englewood Cliffs, NJ: Prentice-Hall, 1984.

Kernighan, B. W. and Ritchie, D. M. *The C Programming Language*. Englewood Cliffs, NJ: Prentice-Hall, 1978.

Kim, Won. On optimizing an SQL-like nested query. *ACM Transactions on Database Systems*, vol. 7, no. 3 (September 1982) : 443–469.

Kim, W., Reiner, D., and Batory, D. Eds. *Query Processing in Database Systems*. NY: Springer-Verlag, 1985.

Korth, Henry F. and Silberschatz, Abraham. *Database System Concepts*. NY: McGraw-Hill, Inc. 1986.

Lewis, H. R., and Papadimitrious, C. H. *Elements of the Theory of Computation*. Englewood Cliffs, NJ: Prentice Hall, 1981.

Lipski, W., Jr. On semantic issues connected with incomplete information databases. *ACM TODS* 4, no. 3 (September 1979).

Maier, David. *The Theory of Relational Databases*. Rockville, MD: Computer Science Press, 1983.

Makkai, Michael and Reyes, Gonzalo E. First order categorical logic. In *Lecture Notes in Mathematics*. Eds. A. Dold and B. Eckmann. NY: Springer-Verlag, 1977.

Marcus, Claudia. *Prolog Programming*. Menlo Park, CA: Addison-Wesley, 1986.

Mendelson, Elliott. *Mathematical Logic*. Princeton, NJ: D. Van Nostrand Company, Inc., 1964.

Nauer, P. Report on the algorithmic language ALGOL 60*. *Communications of the ACM*, 6.1 (1963): 1–17.

Seibert, Graham H. *Working with ORACLE Development Tools*. Blue Ridge Summit, PA: Windcrest Books, 1991.

SQL Plus User's Guide*. Belmont, CA: Oracle Corporation, 1987.

Tarski, A. *Logic, Semantics, Metamathematics*. Oxford University Press, 1956.

Ullman, Jeffrey D. Implementation of logical query languages for databases. *ACM Transactions on Database Systems*, vol. 19, no. 3 (September 1985): 289–321.

Vossen, Gottfried. *Data Models, Database Languages and Database Managements Systems*. Menlo Park, CA: Addison-Wesley, 1990.

Webb, Kenneth and Lori LaFreniere. *ORACLE Distributed Systems: A C Programmer's Development Guide*. Blue Ridge Summit, PA: Windcrest Books, 1991.

Welty, Charles and Stemple, David W. Human factors comparison of a procedural and a nonprocedural query language. *ACM Transactions on Database Systems*, vol. 6, no. 4 (December 1981): 626–649.

Yang, Chao-Chih. *Relational Databases*. Englewood Cliffs, NJ: Prentice Hall, 1986.

Index